ANTIGUA

There are more than one hundred Rough
Guide travel, phrasebook, and music titles,
covering destinations from Amsterdam to
Zimbabwe, languages from Czech to Thai,
and musics from World to Opera and Jazz

Forthcoming titles include

Central America • Japan
Chile • Music USA
Country Music

Rough Guides on the Internet

www.roughguides.com

Rough Guide Credits

Text editor: Chris Schüler   Series editor: Mark Ellingham
Typesetting: Henry Iles   Production: Helen Ostick
Cartography: Maxine Burke

Publishing Information

This first edition published November 1998 by
Rough Guides Ltd, 62–70 Shorts Gardens, London, WC2H 9AB

Distributed by the Penguin Group:

Penguin Books Ltd, 27 Wrights Lane, London W8 5TZ
Penguin Books USA Inc., 375 Hudson Street, New York 10014, USA
Penguin Books Australia Ltd, 487 Maroondah Highway,
PO Box 257, Ringwood, Victoria 3134, Australia
Penguin Books Canada Ltd, 10 Alcorn Avenue,
Toronto, Ontario, Canada M4V 1E4
Penguin Books (NZ) Ltd, 182–190 Wairau Road,
Auckland 10, New Zealand

Typeset in Bembo and Helvetica to an original design by Henry Iles.
Printed in Spain by Graphy Cems.

© Adam Vaitilingam 176pp, includes index
A catalog record for this book is available from the British Library.
ISBN 1-85828-346-9

ANTIGUA

THE MINI ROUGH GUIDE

by Adam Vaitilingam

We set out to do something different when the first Rough Guide was published in 1982. Mark Ellingham, just out of university, was travelling in Greece. He brought along the popular guides of the day, but found they were all lacking in some way. They were either strong on ruins and museums but went on for pages without mentioning a beach or taverna. Or they were so conscious of the need to save money that they lost sight of Greece's cultural and historical significance. Also, none of the books told him anything about Greece's contemporary life – its politics, its culture, its people, and how they lived.

So with no job in prospect, Mark decided to write his own guidebook, one which aimed to provide practical information that was second to none, detailing the best beaches and the hottest clubs and restaurants, while also giving hard-hitting accounts of every sight, both famous and obscure, and providing up-to-the-minute information on contemporary culture. It was a guide that encouraged independent travellers to find the best of Greece, and was a great success, getting shortlisted for the Thomas Cook travel guide award, and encouraging Mark, along with three friends, to expand the series.

The Rough Guide list grew rapidly and the letters flooded in, indicating a much broader readership than had been anticipated, but one which uniformly appreciated the Rough Guide mix of practical detail and humour, irreverence and enthusiasm. Things haven't changed. The same four friends who began the series are still the caretakers of the Rough Guide mission today: to provide the most reliable, up-to-date and entertaining information to independent-minded travellers of all ages, on all budgets.

We now publish more than 100 titles and have offices in London and New York. The travel guides are written and researched by a dedicated team of more than 100 authors, based in Britain, Europe, the USA and Australia. We have also created a unique series of phrasebooks to accompany the travel series, along with an acclaimed series of music guides, and a best-selling pocket guide to the Internet and World Wide Web. We also publish comprehensive travel information on our Web site: **www.roughguides.com**

917.2974
V198
c1

Help Us Update

We've gone to a lot of effort to ensure that this first edition of *The Rough Guide to Antigua* is as up to date and accurate as possible. However, if you feel there are places we've underrated or over-praised, or find we've missed something good or covered something which has now gone, then please write: suggestions, comments or corrections are much appreciated.

We'll credit all contributions, and send a copy of the next edition (or any other Rough Guide if you prefer) for the best letters. Please mark letters: "Rough Guide Antigua Update" and send to:

Rough Guides, 62–70 Shorts Gardens, London WC2 9AB, or
Rough Guides, 375 Hudson St, 9th floor, New York NY 10014.

Or send email to: mail@roughguides.co.uk
Online updates about this book can be found on
Rough Guides' Web site (see opposite)

The Author

Adam Vaitilingam is a barrister and freelance writer who lived in the West Indies from 1989 to 1993. He is the author of the Mini Rough Guide to Barbados, and co-author of the Rough Guide to Jamaica.

Acknowledgements

Thanks to everyone at the Antigua Tourism Office, in London and St John's. Thanks also to Skanda, who first took me to see Viv Richards' bat.

CONTENTS

Introduction

Famous for its beaches and its cricket players, tiny **Antigua** is rapidly becoming one of the Caribbean's most popular destinations. Quiet, unvisited and little-known just a generation ago, the country has taken full advantage of the publicity gained from its independence in 1981 – and the remarkable success of its cricketers since then – to push its name into the big league of West Indian tourism alongside Barbados and Jamaica.

Antigua's early European settlers came from Britain in the sixteenth century. They brought African slaves to clear the native vegetation and plant sugarcane: for centuries, the island was little more than a giant sugar factory, producing sugar and rum to send home to an increasingly sweet-toothed mother country. Around Antigua, the tall brick chimneys of a hundred deserted and decaying sugar mills bear witness to that long colonial era. Today, though, it is tourism that drives the country's economy; dozens of **hotels** and **restaurants** have sprung up around the coast-line, there's a smart new airport, and people offer **boat** and **catamaran cruises** and **scuba diving** and **snorkelling** trips to the island's fabulous coral reefs.

If all you want to do is crash out on a **beach** for a week or two, you'll find Antigua hard to beat. The island is dot-

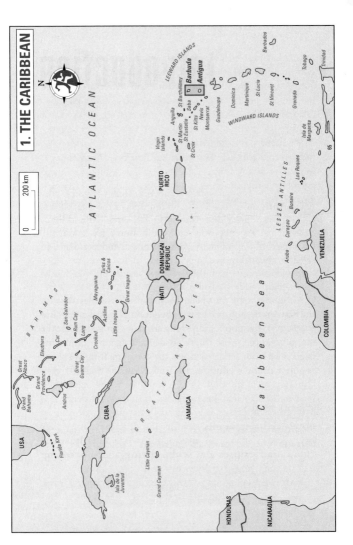

1. THE CARIBBEAN

ted with superb patches of sand - look out for **Dickenson Bay** in the northwest, **Half Moon Bay** in the east and **Rendezvous Beach** in the south - and, while the nightlife is generally pretty quiet, there are plenty of great places to eat and drink. But however lazy you're feeling, it's worth making the effort to get out and see some of the country. The superbly restored naval dockyard and the crumbling forts around **English Harbour** and **Shirley Heights** are as impressive as any historic site in the West Indies, and there are lots of other little nuggets to explore, including the capital, **St John's,** with its tiny museum and colourful quayside, and the old sugar estate at **Betty's Hope**. And, if you're prepared to do a bit of walking, you'll find some superb **hikes** that will take you out to completely deserted parts of the island.

Antigua's sister island **Barbuda** feels a world apart from its increasingly developed neighbour, even though it's just fifteen minutes away by plane. Despite its spectacular beaches and coral reefs, tourism is very low-key; for the island's tiny population, the pace of life seems to have changed little over the generations, and fishing is still the main occupation. Even if you can only manage a day-trip, you'll find it thoroughly repays the effort involved in organizing a tour.

When to go

For many visitors, Antigua's leading attraction is its **tropical climate**: hot and sunny all year round. The weather is at its best during the high season, from mid-December to mid-April, with rainfall low and the heat tempered by cooling trade winds. Things can get noticeably hotter during the summer and, particularly in September and October, the humidity can become oppressive. September is also the most threatening month of the annual hurricane season, which runs officially from June 1 to October 31, though it's worth bearing in mind that, on average, the big blows only hit about once a decade.

As you'd expect, prices and crowds are at their peak during high season, when the main attractions and beaches can get pretty packed. Outside this period everywhere is a little quieter, flight and accommodation prices come down (often dramatically) and you'll find more scope for negotiation on other items.

Antigua's climate

| | °F | | °C | | Rainfall | |
| | Average daily | | Average daily | | Average monthly | |
	max	min	max	min	in	mm
Jan	82	70	28	21	4.8	122
Feb	83	70	33	21	3.4	86
March	85	70	29	21	4.4	112
April	86	72	30	22	3.5	89
May	88	74	31	23	3.8	97
June	88	75	31	24	4.4	112
July	87	75	31	24	6.1	155
Aug	88	75	31	24	7.2	183
Sept	89	74	32	23	6.6	168
Oct	87	74	31	23	7.7	196
Nov	85	73	29	23	7.1	180
Dec	83	72	28	22	5.5	140

Hurricane Georges

In September 1998, just as this book was going to press, Hurricane Georges tore through the Caribbean at speeds of up to 200kph, causing widepread damage from Antigua to the Florida Keys. Fortunately, Antigua's tourist infrastructure appears to have been less seriously disrupted than it was in the aftermath of 1995's Hurricane Luis (see p.53). The airport and telecommunications were fully functioning within a day, and although several hotels and resorts were forced to close for repairs, most should have reopened by the time you read this book. Under the circumstances, however, you would be well advised to ring the Antigua Tourist Office (see p.26) and your hotel for an update before setting out.

BASICS

Getting there from Britain and Ireland

Most British and Irish visitors to Antigua are on some form of package tour which includes a charter flight direct to the island. This is the simplest way of going and, even if you plan to travel independently, it's normally the cheapest too. But charters do have their drawbacks, especially if your plans don't fit into their usual two-week straitjacket. As an alternative, a couple of airlines offer direct scheduled flights from London, and you can find similar fares with other carriers that require a stopover in the USA. There are no direct flights from Ireland to Antigua, but there are good connections via London or, on Aer Lingus or Delta, via New York and Miami (see "Getting There from the USA and Canada", p.7).

There are no direct flights to Barbuda; for details on getting there from Antigua, see chapter 5 of the Guide.

Fares, flights and air passes

Most of the discount and specialist travel agents listed on pp.4 & 6 can quote **fares** on scheduled and charter flights, although some (including Campus, STA and USIT, which all specialize in youth and **student fares**) only quote for scheduled flights. Other useful sources of information are the ads in London's *Time Out* magazine and the travel pages in the *Observer* and other Sunday newspapers. Teletext and Ceefax are also worth a look, as is your local travel agent.

Airlines and discount agents

Airlines

Aer Lingus Dublin ℡01/844 4777; Northern Ireland ℡0645/737747
Air UK Leisure ℡0345/666777
American Airlines ℡0345/789789
British Airways ℡0345/222111
BWIA ℡0181/577 1100
Caledonian Airlines *tickets through the Golden Lion agency,* ℡01293 56800.
Delta Airlines ℡0800/414767; Belfast ℡01232/480526
Virgin Atlantic ℡01293/747747

Discount agents

Budget Travel Dublin ℡01/661 1403
Campus Travel ℡0171/730 8111
Caribbean Travel ℡0181/969 6230
Council Travel ℡0171/437 7767
Flightbookers ℡0171/757 2080
Joe Walsh Tours Dublin ℡01/671 8751; Cork ℡021/277959
The London Flight Centre ℡0171/244 6411
New Look Travel ℡0181/965 8212
Newmont Travel ℡0171/254 6546
Redfern Travel ℡01274/733551
STA Travel ℡0171/361 6262
Trailfinders London ℡0171/938 3366; Dublin ℡01/677 7888
USIT Belfast ℡01232/324073; Dublin ℡01/602 1600

Regardless of where you buy your ticket, fares will depend on the season. These vary from airline to airline, but mid-

December to mid–April is generally classified as high season, and the rest of the year low season. In July and August, however, mid-priced shoulder season fares come into play.

British Airways fly from London Gatwick three times per week, and BWIA fly to the island twice a week from London Heathrow. Return fares with both airlines start at between £400 and £500 in low season, reaching £700–800 in high season. It's often cheaper, if less convenient, to change planes in the US, normally in Miami (see p.8). Delta, Virgin, British Airways and American Airlines all fly from London to Miami, with fares as low as £200–250 during the low season.

Charter operators Caledonian Airlines, Britannia and Monarch all fly from London, and Airtours also fly from Manchester. They are normally significantly cheaper than scheduled flights, but tend to arrive and depart at anti-social hours, and there is little or no flexibility once the ticket is booked. Fares start at as little as £199 during low season, rising to £500+ in high season. Most charter flights are for a fortnight, though you can also find charters for one or three weeks.

Finally, if you fancy visiting more than one Caribbean island, BWIA and the eastern Caribbean airline LIAT offer **air passes**, available in Britain, which allow you to do just that (see p.19).

Packages and tours

A **package holiday** can offer excellent value, and often works out much cheaper than arranging separate flights, transfers and accommodation yourself. There are all kinds of deals available, depending on whether you opt for an all-inclusive (hotel room plus all meals), room only, or self-catering option (usually a hotel room with simple cooking facilities). Most packages are for two weeks, and you may have to shop around to find a one-week or three-week deal.

All-inclusive packages at a three-star hotel start at around £700 per person for a week, £950 for a fortnight, based on double occupancy, while room-only and self-catering deals start at around £450 per person for a week, £500 for a fortnight, again based on two people sharing. All deals include the flight and transfers from airport to hotel.

A handful of tour operators offer **specialized tours** based, for example, around getting married or catching the West Indies cricket season. And if you want to see Antigua for a day, you could do worse than a Caribbean cruise; these start at around £1000, including a return flight to the embarkation point in Miami (see p.10).

Specialist package and tour operators

Airtours ✆01706/240033
Calypso Gold ✆0181/977 9655
Caribtours ✆0171/581 3517
Cosmos Travel ✆0181/464 3444
Hayes and Jarvis ✆0181/748 008
Joe Walsh Tours Dublin ✆01/676 3053
Kuoni Travel ✆01306/742222
Thomas Cook Britain ✆0990/666222;
Belfast ✆01232/242341; Dublin ✆01/677 1721
Thomson Holidays ✆0171/387 9321
Tropical Places ✆01342/825123

Getting there from the USA and Canada

The most obvious way of getting to Antigua is **by air**. There are few cheap flights to Antigua, however, and the airlines usually don't offer special student rates or air passes. Nor does the Caribbean fit too well into a round-the-world (RTW) itinerary. For more leisurely transport, several **cruise ships** call at the island, and it is even possible to sail there by **yacht** from Florida.

Fares and flights

Apart from special promotions, the cheapest published fare is usually an **APEX ticket**, although you have to book – and pay – at least 21 days before departure, spend at least seven days abroad, and you tend to get penalized if you change your schedule.

You can normally cut costs further by going through a consolidator or a discount agent, who may also offer **student and youth fares** and a range of other services such as travel insurance, rail passes, car rentals, and tours. Penalties for changing your plans can be stiff, however. Some agents specialize in **charter flights**, which may be cheaper than any scheduled flight, but again departure dates are fixed and withdrawal penalties are high.

Airlines in the USA and Canada

American Airlines ✆1-800/433-7300
American Eagle ✆1-800/433-7300
Air Canada ✆1-800/776-3000
BWIA ✆1-800/538-2942
Continental Airlines ✆1-800/525-0280 domestic;
✆1-800/231-0856 international

Discount travel agents and consolidators

Council Travel ✆1-800/226-8624
STA Travel ✆1-800/777-0112 or ✆212/627-3111
Travel CUTS ✆1-800/667-2887 Canada only or
✆416/979-2406
Worldtek Travel ✆1-800/243-1723 or ✆203/772-0470

Regardless of where you buy your ticket, fares will depend on the season. Definitions vary from airline to airline, but **high season** generally extends from mid-December to late April and from the end of June to mid-September. The rest of the year is considered **low season**.

The following are typical high/low season APEX fares, departing mid-week, from US/Canadian cities to VC Bird International Airport in Antigua: New York (US$605/470); Atlanta, (US$760/705); Chicago (US$800/745); Los Angeles (US$952/898); Miami (US$569/516); Toronto (CAN$869/724).

American Airlines offers the best fares and most comprehensive schedule from the United States to Antigua; all of their flights connect either through Miami or San Juan, Puerto Rico. BWIA flies non-stop to Antigua from New York and Miami, while Continental has three weekly non-stop flights out of Newark, New Jersey.

Air Canada offers the best fares out of Toronto, although they only fly to Antigua on Saturdays; American Airlines has a wider range of options at competitive prices. BWIA's direct flight from Toronto, which leaves once a week, is also good value. Getting from Vancouver to Antigua is a challenge since an overnight stay is ususally required to catch a flight from Toronto or one of the US gateways.

Another solution is to fly to San Juan, Puerto Rico and then on to Antigua; American Eagle flies to San Juan nonstop from LA, Dallas, Chicago, Baltimore/Washington Dulles, Miami and Kennedy/Newark. Vancouver via New York to San Juan, for example, costs around CAN$697 year round. Flights from Chicago are (US$802/542) and from New York (US$450/262) in high/low season. From San Juan to Antigua is about US$190 round-trip, year round, though cheaper specials are frequent.

Packages and tours

Although flights from North America to Antigua can be reasonably priced, you can sometimes find an even less expensive alternative with a **vacation package**. Most cover the air fare, transfers, accommodation and airport taxes, and can include meals. Prices start from US$880, leaving from New York or Miami (BWIA Vacations), for seven nights in low season, and generally hover around US$1500 for a two-week stay.

Tour operators

Although phone numbers are given here, you're better off making tour reservations through your local travel agent, who will make all the phone calls, sort out the snafus and arrange flights, insurance and the like at no extra cost.

Air Canada Vacations ✆1-800/774-8993
American Airlines Vacations ✆1-800/321-2121
Alken Tours ✆1-800/221-6686 or ✆718/856-7711
BWIA Vacations ✆1-800/780-5501 or ✆718/520-8100
Friendly Holidays ✆1-800/456-7754

Inter Island Tours ✆1-800/245-3434
Tour Host International ✆1-800/THE HOST or ✆212/953-7910
TourScan Inc ✆1-800/962 2080 or ✆203/655 8091;
www.tourscan.com
Travel Impressions ✆1-800/284-0044

By sea

If you plan to **yacht** to Antigua, the US Coast Guard in Miami will steer you in the right direction (✆305/535 4470), or you can call US Sailing (✆1 800/-US SAIL 1 or ✆401/683 0800).

Cruise operators

The fares quoted below are for **low season** (see p.8) seven-day cruises in single person/double occupancy "inside" (no ocean views) cabins, and are exclusive of port charges which add an extra US$110 to US$150. The cruises stop only once in Antigua and leave from San Juan, Puerto Rico unless otherwise noted.

Docking in St John's

Celebrity Cruises ✆1-800/437-3111; from US$899
Cunard ✆1-800/221-4770; from $5670 for a 16-day cruise from Lisbon to Miami or 7 days on a luxury 116-person "yacht" out of St Thomas from US$6750
Holland American Line ✆1-800/426-0327 or ✆206/281-3535; from US$1592 for a 10-day cruise starting in Ft Lauderdale
Norwegian Cruise Line ✆1-800/327-7030; from US$649
Royal Caribbean International ✆1-800/327-6700; from US$699 including port charges
Royal Olympic ✆1-800/368-3888; 14-day cruises from Ft. Lauderdale to Brazil or vice versa starting at US$1977
Windjammer ✆1-800/327-2601; 6-day round-trip cruise starting and ending in Antigua from US$875

Getting there from Australia and New Zealand

The Caribbean is no bargain destination from Australasia. There are no direct flights from Australia or New Zealand to the island of Antigua, so you'll have to take a flight to one of the main US gateway airports, and pick up onward connections from there.

Generally, the least expensive and most straightforward routes are via New York or Miami, from where there are regular flights to St John's. If you're planning to see Antigua as part of a longer trip, round-the-world (RTW) tickets are worth considering, and are usually better value than a simple return flight. Whatever kind of ticket you're after, first call should be one of the specialist travel agents listed on pp.13–15, which can fill you in on all the latest fares and any special offers. If you're a student or under 26, you may be able to undercut some of the prices given here; STA is a good place to start.

Fares and air passes

All the fares quoted below are for travel during **low or shoulder seasons**, and exclude airport taxes; flying at peak times (primarily Dec to mid-Jan) can add subtsantially to these prices.

The best fares you're likely to find are the Air New Zealand, United and Qantas regular services to Los Angeles, with connecting flights to New York or Miami flying American Airlines or United: return fares to Miami cost around A$2259 from the **eastern states**, rising to A$2699 from **Western Australia**.

From New Zealand, the same airlines fly to Los Angeles, with connections on to Miami or New York; through fares to Miami start at NZ$2799.

Onward flights from New York or Miami to **St John's** cost around A$450/NZ$522 return, flying with BWIA. American Airlines also operate flights from Chicago and Atlanta, via San Juan, at similar prices. (See "Getting there from the USA and Canada" from more on connections from North America.)

If you plan to indulge in some island-hopping around the Caribbean, BWIA or LIAT **air passes** can be worthwhile (see p.19).

RTW tickets

Given these fares and routings, **round-the-world tickets** that take in one of the gateway airports in the United States are worth considering, especially if you have the time to make the most of a few stopovers.

Ultimately, your choice of route will depend on where else you want to visit besides Antigua, but a couple of sample itineraries might whet your appetite. Starting from either **Melbourne, Sydney or Brisbane**, you could fly to Bangkok to Paris to Nice to New York to Los Angeles and then back to Melbourne, Sydney or Brisbane (from A$1999); from **Perth**, you could take in Los Angeles, New York, Paris and Nairobi before heading back to Perth (from A$2299).

Airlines

Air New Zealand, 5 Elizabeth St, Sydney, ©13 2746; 139 Queen St, Auckland, ©09/357 3000.

American Airlines, 8/80 Clarence St, Sydney, ©1300/650 747. No NZ office.

BWIA International Airways, 12/456 Kent St, Sydney, ©02/9223 7004. No NZ office.

Qantas, 70 Hunter St, Sydney, ©13 1211; 154 Queen St, Auckland, ©0800/808 767 or ©09/357 8900.

United Airlines, 5/10 Barrack St, Sydney, ©13 1777; 7 City Rd, Auckland, ©09/379 3800.

Travel agents

Anywhere Travel, 345 Anzac Parade, Kingsford, Sydney, ©02/9663 0411; email: *anywhere@ozemail.com.au*

Brisbane Discount Travel, 260 Queen St, Brisbane, ©07/3229 9211.

Budget Travel, 16 Fort St, Auckland, plus branches around the city, ©09/366 0061 or ©0800/808 040.

Destinations Unlimited, 3 Milford Rd, Auckland, ©09/373 4033.

Flight Centres Australia: 82 Elizabeth St, Sydney, plus branches nationwide, ©13 1600. New Zealand: 205 Queen St, Auckland, ©09/309 6171, plus branches nationwide.

Northern Gateway, 22 Cavenagh St, Darwin, ©08/8941 1394.

STA Travel, Australia: 702 Harris St, Ultimo, Sydney; 256 Flinders St, Melbourne; other offices in state capitals and major universities (nearest branch ©13 1776, fastfare telesales ©1300/360 960). New Zealand: 10 High St, Auckland, ©09/309 0458, fastfare telesales ©09/366 6673, plus branches in Wellington, Christchurch, Dunedin, Palmerston North, Hamilton and at major universities. Web site: *www.statravelaus.com.au*; email: *traveller@statravelaus.com.au*

Thomas Cook, Australia: 175 Pitt St, Sydney; 257 Collins St, Melbourne; plus branches in other state capitals (local branch ✆13 1771, Thomas Cook Direct telesales ✆1800/063 913); New Zealand: 96 Anzac Ave, Auckland, ✆09/379 3920.
Trailfinders, 8 Spring St, Sydney, ✆02/9247 7666.
The Travel Specialists, 80 Clarence St, Sydney, ✆02/9290 1500. Web site: *www.travel.com.au*; email: *consultant@travel.com.au*
Tymtro Travel, 314 Victoria Ave, Chatswood, Sydney, ✆1300/652 969.

Packages and tours

Package holidays from Australia and New Zealand to Antigua are few and far between, and many specialists simply act as **agents** for US-based operators, tagging a return flight from Australasia on to the total cost.

Cruises account for the largest sector of the market: most depart from Miami, and because prices are based on US dollar amounts, they fluctuate with the exchange rate, but to give some idea, all-inclusive three-day cruises start from A$760, while seven-day cruises cost upwards of A$1200. The luxury end of the market is also catered for by Caribbean Destinations and Contours, both of which offer **resort**- and **villa-based holidays** as well as cruises, with a choice of accommodation on Antigua – mostly in fully inclusive resort complexes, such as Club Antigua and Sandals Antigua. Prices start around A$4000 for 14 days (based on twin-share accommodation and low-season air-fares from Australia), but really the sky's the limit.

None of the adventure-tour operators venture to Antigua; for independent travellers, the cheapest way to visit the Caribbean is as part of a **round-the-world** or American holiday, making creative use of air passes – see p.19.

Specialist agents and tour operators

Caribbean Destinations, 4/115 Pitt St, Sydney; 38/525 Collins St, Melbourne, ✆1800/816 717. Comprehensive range of tailor-made Caribbean holidays, including a range of accommodation packages.

Contours, 466 Victoria St, North Melbourne, ✆03/9329 5211. Choice of accommodation-and-airfare package deals to Antigua, as well as other Caribbean destinations.

Creative Tours, 3/55 Grafton St, Woollahra, Sydney, ✆02/9836 2111. Caribbean cruise agents.

Wiltrans, 10/189 Kent St, Sydney, ✆02/9255 0899. Agents for a range of Caribbean cruise operators.

Getting around

A lot of people come to Antigua, make straight for their hotel and spend the next fortnight lying on the beach. For those who want to tour around and see the island, though, there are are a variety of options.

Speedy and inexpensive buses run to certain parts of the island, particularly between St John's and English Harbour on the south coast, but few go near the main tourist areas. If you want to tour around, you're invariably better off renting a **car** for a couple of days – though this isn't cheap. If you just want to make the odd excursion or short trip, it can work out cheaper to hire **taxis**.

GETTING TO AND FROM THE AIRPORT

There is no bus service to and from V.C. Bird International Airport. There are numerous **car rental** outlets at the airport, while **taxis** cost around US$6 to Dickenson Bay or US$25 to English Harbour.

By bus

The public transport system in Antigua is patchy, with **buses** offering fast, frequent and cheap service between St John's and English Harbour, via the centre of the island, and less frequent service to Parham and Willikies on the east coast (from where it's a 15-minute walk to the Long Bay beach). There is no service to the tourist strip of Runaway Bay and Dickenson Bay on the northwest coast, nor to the airport. **Minibuses** run along the west coast between St John's and Old Road, stopping off beside several good beaches and the local hotels en route. For the south and west coasts, buses and minibuses use the West End bus terminal near the main market in St John's; for the east coast, they use the east terminal near the Recreation Ground.

Few of the buses run to any schedule, often departing only where they are reasonably full. Always ask the driver where he's going and tell him well in advance of where you want to get off. Stops are normally marked, though you'll find that the minivans will usually stop anywhere en route. Few buses run after dark or on Sunday.

By car

Antigua is an easy country to **drive** in; the roads are mostly good and distances are small. Driving is on the left. Rental prices, however, are fairly high, starting at around US$45 per day, $250 per week. Third party **insurance** is included in the price; if you don't have a credit card that offers free collision damage insurance, you'll have to pay another US$10–12 per day if you want to cover potential damage to the rental car.

When renting, you'll need to buy a local driving licence for US$20 (valid for three months) and to show a current **licence** from your home country or an international driver's licence. You'll also normally need a **credit card** to make a security deposit. Check the car fully to ensure that every dent, scratch or missing part is inventoried before you set off. When returning the car, don't forget to collect any credit card deposit slip.

Reliable firms include: Avis (©462 2840), Budget (©462 3009), Dollar (©462 0362), Hertz (©462 4114), and Oakland (©462 3021). Each of these can provide you with a car at the airport or deliver to your hotel.

GETTING AROUND

By taxi

Finding a **taxi** in Antigua – identifiable from an H on their numberplates – is easy in St John's, Nelson's Dockyard or at the airport; less straightforward in other areas of the island, where you'll often need to call (or ask your hotel to arrange) for one. Fares are regulated but there are no meters, so make sure that you agree a price before you get into the car. At the airport there is a list of government-approved rates: US$7 to St John's, $6 to Dickenson Bay or Runaway Bay, $25 to English Harbour. If you rent a taxi for a day's sightseeing, expect to pay around US$60–70

Motorbikes and cycling

Since Antigua is so small, and there are few steep inclines, it would seem like ideal **cycling** territory, yet this mode of transport has never really caught on, and there are few outlets for cycle hire. Hiring a scooter or **motorbike** is a little easier – prices normally start at around US$20 per day (plus $20 for the local driving permit) – and can be a fantastic way of touring around, though you'll need to watch out for madcap drivers on the main roads. Rental agents for bikes include Cycle Krazy, St Mary's Street in St John's (✆462 9253) and Sun Cycles in Hodges Bay (✆461 0324); for motorbikes try JT's Rent-a-Scoot in Parham Town (✆463 3578).

Tours

In case you don't fancy driving, there are a couple of local companies who offer island-wide **sight-seeing tours**, either to a set itinerary or customized to your needs. Remember to check whether the price includes entrance fees to the various attractions. Your hotel may also organize tours direct. If you can't get a good price from any of the companies below, you could check with some of the taxi operators listed in the individual chapters.

Tropikelly Trails (©461 0383) offer 5 to 6-hour tours from US$55 including a picnic lunch per person, with trips to Great George Fort, Boggy Peak and a pineapple farm. Antours (©462 4788) and Bo Tours (©462 6632) also offer tours to the island's main sights, including English Harbour and Betty's Hope at a similar cost.

For tours to Barbuda, see chapter 5 of the Guide.

Yachting charters

Charters can be arranged through Sun Yacht Charters (©460 2615) or Nicholson's Yacht Charters (©460 1530), both at English Harbour.

VISITING OTHER ISLANDS

LIAT (©462 0700) are based in Antigua and run **flights** to virtually all of the Caribbean islands as well as into Venezuela in South America. Fares start at around US$75 for round-trip flights to Montserrat or Anguilla; longer haul flights start at around US$100, but most will allow you one or more free stopovers en route. Tickets are sold at a multitude of travel agents island-wide. Carib Airlines (©462 3147) offer local charters, and can work out cheaper than LIAT for a group of 5 to 9 people.

If you fancy a spot of island hopping, BWIA and LIAT both sell **air passes** that allow for multiple trips around the Caribbean on their airline only. LIAT's is the best value at $US80, allowing you to stop off at any of their destinations in a 21-day period. You can take as many flights as you want, as long as each country is only visited once. The pass can only be bought outside the Caribbean in conjunction with a long-distance air ticket. BWIA's 30-day air pass costs $US399, and covers fewer islands. You may visit each country once, but your route is restricted.

GETTING AROUND

Visas and red tape

Citizens of Britain, Ireland, the US, Canada, Australia and New Zealand can enter Antigua without a **visa** and stay for up to six months. You will, however, need a **passport** (valid for at least six months after the date of onward travel) and a return ticket or proof of onward travel. You might also be asked to show that you have sufficient funds to cover your stay; if you can't satisfy the immigration authorities, they have the right to deny you entry. You will also be asked where you intend to stay, though your answer will not of course be binding. There is no fee for entering Antigua, but you will have to pay a US$13 departure tax when you leave.

Antiguan embassies and consulates

UK 1 Great Russell St, London WC1B 3JY, ℡0171/631 4975.
US 3216 New Mexico Ave NW, Washington DC 20016, ℡202/362 5122.
Canada 105 Adelaide St West, Suite 1010, Toronto, Ontario M5H 1P9, ℡ 416/214 9805.
There is no Antiguan embassy or consulate in Ireland, Australia or New Zealand.

Foreign embassies in Antigua

British High Commission, 11 Old Parham Rd, St John's, ℡462 0008.
There are no US, Canadian or Australian embassies or commissions in Antigua.

Health and insurance

If you need medical or dental treatment on the island, you'll find the standard reasonably high. St John's has the 225-bed public **Holberton Hospital** (℡462 0251) on its eastern outskirts, while smaller health centres and clinics are distributed around the island. For an ambulance, call ℡462 0251.

Before buying an insurance policy, check that you're not already covered. Private health plans typically provide some **overseas medical coverage**, although they are unlikely to pick up the full tab in the event of a mishap. Homeowners' or renters' insurance often covers theft or loss of documents, money and valuables while overseas. After exhausting these possibilities, you might want to contact a specialist travel insurance company; your travel agent can usually recommend one (or see p.24).

Health

Travelling in Antigua is usually very safe as far as **health** is concerned. Food is invariably well and hygienically prepared and the tapwater is safe to drink.

No jabs are needed – the major tropical diseases were eradicated long ago – and you'll find that the only real threat to your physical welfare is the intense **Caribbean sun**. Many visitors get badly sunburned on the first day and suffer for the rest of the trip – you'll see them peeling around the island. To avoid their fate, it's advisable to wear a strong sunscreen at all times; if you're after a tan, start strong and gradually reduce the factor. As for exposure times, 15 minutes a day in the early morning or late afternoon is recommended, if rarely followed; unreconstructed sun-worshippers should at least avoid the heat of the day between 11.30am and 2.30pm. For the sunburned, aloe vera gel is available at the island's pharmacies.

While you're on the beach, steer clear of the **manchi-neel trees**, recognizable by their shiny green leaves and the small, crab apple-like fruits scattered around on the ground. The fruit is poisonous and, when it rains, the bark gives off a poisonous sap which will cause blisters if it drips on you. The sea, too, poses a handful of threats. Don't worry about the rarely seen sharks or barracudas, which won't spoil your visit, but watch out for spiny black **sea urchins**. They're easily missed if you're walking over a patch of sea grass; if you step on one and can't get the spines out, you'll need medical help. Finally, mosquitos and tiny sandflies can be an occasional problem, particularly on the beach in late afternoon; take **insect repellent** to keep them at bay.

Insurance

Most people will find it essential to take out a good **travel insurance policy** for a trip to Antigua, ideally covering at least medical treatment, theft and loss of baggage. Check first, though, to find out if you already have any coverage: bank and credit cards (particularly American Express) often have certain levels of medical or other insurance included if you use them to pay for your trip; this can be quite comprehensive, anticipating such mishaps as lost or stolen baggage, missed connections and charter companies going bust. Similarly, if you have a good "all risks" home insurance policy, it may well cover your possessions against loss or theft even when overseas, and many private medical schemes also cover you when abroad – make sure you know the procedure and the relevant telephone number. If you're planning a trip to mainland South America, make sure that your insurance extends to the region.

If you plan to participate in **water sports**, you may have to pay an extra premium; check carefully that any insurance policy you are considering will cover you in case of an accident. Note also that very few insurers will arrange on-the-spot payments in the event of a major expense or loss; you will usually be reimbursed only after going home.

In all cases of loss or **theft** of goods, you will have to contact the local police to have a report made out so that your insurer can process the claim; for **medical claims**, you'll need to provide receipts and supporting bills. If you are going to make a claim, make a note of any time period within which you must lodge it, and keep photocopies of everything you send to the insurer.

British and Irish cover

In Britain and Ireland, travel insurance schemes (from around £35 a month for Antigua) are sold by almost every travel agent or bank, and by specialist insurance companies. Policies issued by Campus Travel, STA, Endsleigh, Frizzell or Columbus (see overleaf for details) are all good value. Columbus and some banks also do multi-trip policies which offer twelve months' cover for around £90.

North American cover

Premiums for travel to Antigua start at around US$65 for a two-week trip; $85 for three weeks to a month. Longer-term plans are also available. Note that most North American travel policies apply only to items lost, stolen or damaged while in the custody of an identifiable, responsible third party – hotel porter, airline, luggage consignment, etc. Even in these cases, you will have to contact the local police within a certain time limit to have a complete report made out so that your insurer can process the claim.

Australian and New Zealand cover

Travel insurance is available from travel agents or direct from insurance companies (see below) Policies are broadly comparable in premium and coverage; a typical one will cost A$190/NZ$220 for one month.

Travel insurance suppliers

Britain and Ireland

Campus Travel ✆0171/730 8111
Columbus Travel Insurance ✆0171/375 0011
Endsleigh Insurance ✆0171/436 4451
Frizzell Insurance ✆01202/292333
STA ✆0171/361 6262
USIT Belfast ✆01232/324073; Dublin ✆01/679 8833

USA and Canada

Access America ✆1-800/284-8300
Carefree Travel Insurance ✆1-800/645-2424
Desjardins Travel Insurance (Canada only) ✆1-800/463-7830
ISIS (International Student Insurance Service) – sold by STA Travel ✆1-800/777-0112
Travel Assistance International ✆1-800/821-2828
Travel Guard ✆1-800/826-1300
Travel Insurance Services ✆1-800/937 1387

Australia and New Zealand

AFTA ✆02/9956 4800
Cover More, in Sydney ✆02/9968 1333; elsewhere in Australia toll-free ✆1800/251881
Ready Plan Australia toll-free ✆1800/337462; New Zealand ✆09/379 3399
UTAG, in Sydney ✆02/9819 6855; elsewhere in Australia, toll-free ✆1900/809462

Information and maps

Before you leave home, you may want to contact the **Antigua Tourist Office** (ATO) nearest you. Their offices stock plenty of information on the country, including brochures on the main tourist attractions and forthcoming events, and a good road map. Once you're in Antigua, you can get the same information from the ATO office on Long and Thames streets in St John's (①462 0029) or from their desk at the airport. Most of the car rental outlets will also provide you with a free map of the island when you rent from them.

Antigua on the Internet

antigua-barbuda.com
The official Web site of Antigua and Barbuda, aimed largely at attracting foreign business investment.

www.skyviews.com/antigua
The Antigua page of the useful and informative Caribbean Web site Calabash Skyviews has information on watersports, eating and accommodation.

http://www.cinesecrets.com/AntiguaPage/cfAntiguaFrame.html
www.cinesecrets.com/poIslandArtsDoor.html
Two lively pages by artist, film-effects creator and Antiguan resident Nick Maley, one devoted to the island's culture and sights, the other to his Island Arts gallery (see p.54).

Antigua has no detailed listings magazine for music, theatre and other events, though the *Antigua Sun* daily newspaper carries details of many of the events. Keep an eye also on flyers posted up around the island; local radio stations (see p.31) also advertise major events.

Antigua tourist offices overseas

Britain Antigua House, 15 Thayer St, London W1M 5LD, ✆0171 486 7073, fax 0171 486 9970.
Canada 60 St Clair Ave East, Suite 304, Toronto, Ontario M4T IN5, ✆416 961 3085, fax 961 7218.
USA 610 5th Avenue, Suite 311, New York NY 10020, ✆212-541 4117, fax 757 1607; 25 SE 2nd Avenue, Suite 300, Miami, Florida 33131, ✆305-381 6762, fax 305-381 7908.
(The ATO has no branches in Australia or New Zealand)

Money and costs

Antigua is not a particularly cheap country to visit, and prices for many items are at least as much as you'd pay at home. Negotiation on price is generally frowned on – taxi rates, for example, are normally fixed – but, particularly during the off-season of April to November, it can be worth asking for a reduced rate for items such as accommodation or car rental.

Currency

The island's unit of currency is the **Eastern Caribbean dollar** (EC$), divided into 100 cents. It comes in bills of $100, $50, $20, $10 and $5 and coins of $1, $0.50, $0.25, $0.10, $0.05 and $0.01. The rate of exchange is fixed at EC$2.70 to US$1 (giving you, at the time of writing, roughly EC$4.2 to UK£1), though you'll get a fraction less when you exchange money. In tourist-related business, the US$ is often used as an unofficial parallel currency, and you'll often find prices for hotels, restaurants and car rental quoted in US$ (a policy we have adopted in this guide). You can always insist on paying in EC$ (and the exchange rate usually works out slightly in your favour) but you may find it easier in such places to use your US dollars, travellers' cheques or credit cards. If you are using US dollars or travellers' cheques to pay a bill, check in advance whether your change will be given in the same currency (it usually won't).

Costs

Apart from the flight, **accommodation** is likely to be the major expense of your trip. Double rooms start at around US$25, though most of the cheaper options cost around US$35–40 in winter, $30–35 in summer. For something more salubrious, expect to pay at least $70–80 in winter, $50–60 in summer. Rooms apart, if you **travel** around on foot and by bus and get your **food** from supermarkets and the cheaper cafés, you could just about survive on a **daily budget** of around US$15 per day. Upgrading to one decent meal out, the occasional taxi ride and a bit of evening entertainment, expect to spend a more realistic US$30–35 per day; after that, the sky's the limit.

Travellers' cheques and plastic

Easily the safest and most convenient method of carrying money abroad is in the form of **travellers' cheques** and, while sterling and other currencies are perfectly valid and accepted in the island's banks, US dollars travellers' cheques are the best ones to have. They are available for a small commission from most banks, and from branches of American Express and Thomas Cook; make sure you keep the purchase agreement and a record of cheque serial numbers safe and separate from the cheques themselves. Once in Antigua, they can be cashed at banks (you'll need your passport or other photo ID to validate them) for a small charge.

Major credit cards – American Express, Visa, Mastercard – are widely accepted, but don't necessarily expect the smaller hotels and restaurants to take them. You can also use the cards to get cash advances at most banks, though you'll pay both commission to the bank and hefty interest to your credit card company.

Banking hours are generally Mon–Thurs 8am–3pm, Friday 8am–5pm; branches of the Caribbean Commercial Bank are also open on Saturday from 9am–noon. Many **hotels** will also exchange money, though if you're changing anything other than US$ the rate is usually a bit worse than the banks (see p.129).

Emergency cash

If you **run out** of money, you can arrange a telegraphic transfer to most of the banks in Antigua from your home bank account or that of a friend or family member. Bear in mind that such a transfer will attract hefty commission at both ends, so treat this very much as a last resort.

Communications and the media

Antigua's **postal service** is reasonably efficient. The GPO in St John's is open Mon–Fri 8.15am–noon and 1-5pm (5pm Fri) and has poste restante facilities for receiving mail. There are also branches at the airport, at the Woods Centre and at English Harbour, and you can buy stamps and send mail at many of the hotels. **Postal rates** are reasonable: to the UK, USA and Canada, air mail EC$0.90, postcards EC$0.45; to Australasia, air mail EC$1.20, postcards $0.60.

Calling within Antigua is simple – most hotels provide a **telephone** in each room. You'll also see **phone booths** all over the island, and these can be used for local and international calls. Most of the booths take phonecards only – they're available at hotels, post offices and some shops and supermarkets. For finding numbers, hotel rooms and phone booths often have a directory; failing that, call directory assistance on ℂ411. To reach the operator dial 0.

International calls

Phoning Antigua from abroad

Dial your international access code (see below) + 268 + seven-digit number

UK ℂ001

USA ℂ011

Canada ©011
Australia ©0011
New Zealand ©00

Phoning abroad from Antigua

Dial country code (see below) + area code minus first 0 +
number
UK ©011 44
USA ©1
Canada ©1
Australia ©011 61
New Zealand ©011 64

Press, radio and TV

As always, local newspapers and radio are a great way to
find out what's on the nation's mind. The daily *Antigua Sun*
is the best paper, concentrating on domestic news but with
a decent section on news from the wider Caribbean and the
rest of the world and, invariably, a big sports section. The
main radio stations are the public service channel **ABS** (620
AM), and the commercial **Sun FM** (100.1 FM). They both
carry news, sport, chat shows and music, mostly international hits with a sprinkling of local tunes.

Festivals, events and public holidays

The main events in Antigua are the summertime **Carnival** (see p.117), and the April Sailing Week, but there are various other events to distract you from the beach, including international **cricket** and **windsurfing** tournaments, and a **jazz festival**. The local and overseas tourist boards (see p.25) have full details of all the activities.

Annual events

Jan	**Red Stripe Cricket Competition**	✆462 9090
Feb	**Valentine's Regatta**, Jolly Harbour	✆462 7595
Mar–Apr	**Test cricket**	✆462 9090
April	**Classic Regatta**	✆460 1444
	Sailing Week	✆460 1444
May	**Pro-Am Tennis Classic**	
	Curtain Bluff Hotel	✆462 8400
Aug	**Carnival** see p.117	
Oct	**Jazz festival**	
Nov	**Antiguan Craft Fair** Harmony Hall	
Dec	**Nicholson's Annual Charter -**	
	Yacht Show,	✆460 1444

Public holidays

New Year's Day	Jan 1
Good Friday	
Easter Monday	
Labour Day	first Mon in May
Whit Monday	end of May
Caricom Day	early July
Carnival	first Mon and Tues in Aug
United Nations Day	first Mon in Oct
Independence Day	Nov 1
Christmas Day	Dec 25
Boxing Day	Dec 26

FESTIVALS, EVENTS AND PUBLIC HOLIDAYS

Shopping

If you want to take home something authentically Antiguan, check out the stores and **craft stalls** around Redcliffe Quay and Heritage Quay in St John's (see p.42), or wait for the vendors to find you – those on the most popular beaches, particularly Dickenson Bay on the northwest coast, regularly set up stands selling clothing, carved wooden figurines and Haitian-style paintings of markets and other traditional scenes. There are also some excellent art stores and plenty of T-shirt and craft vendors at Nelson's Dockyard on the south coast.

Other than that, you're largely restricted to the familiar **duty-free** options, with a massive array at Heritage Quay (see p.43). If you're after duty-free liquor, jewellery, clothes, cameras or perfume, you'll find all the shops you need there (Mon–Sat 9am–5pm and Sun when there's a cruise ship in port). Take your passport of air ticket as proof of visitor status.

The island's main shopping mall is the modern **Woods Centre**, just outside St John's (see p.50), where you'll find the island's best-equipped supermarkets, pharmacies, bookshops and numerous other stores. For general food shopping, grocery stores are dotted around the island, while the market in St John's is the most colourful place to visit (see p.47), particularly on Saturday morning when it hums with life and stands are piled high with yams, mangos, paw-paws and other fruit and vegetables; there are fish and meat sections too.

SHOPPING

Drugs, trouble and harassment

Compared to what you'll encounter in Jamaica or several other Caribbean islands, **harassment** in Antigua is extremely mild. The itinerant vendors who patrol some of the beaches are the main culprits – you'll occasionally be offered drugs or pressed to look at some uninspiring crafts – but on the whole a recent police crackdown has kept them at a distance. If you're not interested, just be firm in saying no thanks and they'll leave you alone.

Violent crime involving tourists is rare but not unheard of. After dark, it's advisable to steer clear of unlit or unpatrolled areas of the beach, and you'll probably want to avoid the rougher areas of Antigua (see pp.40–41), though there's no reason why you'd want to visit them. **Drugs** present an increasing problem on the island, particularly a growing use of crack cocaine, which is leading to a rise in theft and burglary to finance the habit. Marijuana use is just as widespread – and equally illegal – often distributed on the beaches, particularly on the south coast, to likely-looking punters. If you want it, you can get it, but bear in mind that there are plenty of undercover police around, and the local press runs stories daily of tourists facing heavy fines for possession.

Emergency numbers

Police ✆462 0125 • **Fire** ✆462 0044 • **Ambulance** ✆462 0251

THE GUIDE

St John's and around

With a population of around 30,000 – nearly half the island's total – bustling **St John's** is Antigua's capital and only city. No one could accuse it of being the prettiest city in the West Indies, but it does have a certain immediate charm and, in the centre, there are plenty of attractive old wooden and stone buildings – some of them superbly renovated, others in a perilous state of near-collapse – among the less appealing modern development. It'll only take you a couple of hours to see everything but, even if you're not staying in the capital, you'll probably want to come back for an evening or two to take advantage of some excellent **restaurants** and **bars** as well as the city's **nightlife**.

There's no beach to speak of in St John's but, a short ride away, **Fort Bay** has a lovely stretch of sand, absolutely packed at weekends and on holidays, while nearby **Fort James** is one of the best-preserved colonial forts on the island. The fort overlooks (and once protected) the narrow channel of water that has taken trading ships into the city's harbour for over 300 years.

Getting there and getting around

As all of the main places of interest in St John's are close together, the easiest way to see the place is **on foot**. Driving in the city is straightforward if not particularly enjoyable; parking space is limited, the one-way traffic system is a little tricky to deal with, and potholes and roadside rain gullies threaten damage to your car at every turn. You'll be offered **taxis** virtually wherever you go but, for the record, there are taxi stands just west of the market at the southern end of town, beside the east bus station near the Antigua Recreation Ground, and at Heritage Quay.

If you're arriving in or leaving the city by **bus**, the east bus station serves the north of the island (Dickenson Bay, Cedar Grove and the airport) and the east (Pares and Willikies), while the west bus station, beside the market, serves the west (Five Islands) and south (Jolly Harbour, Old Road, Falmouth and English Harbour).

Information

The government's main **tourist office** (℗462 0480) is on the corner of Thames Street and Long Street, and has a perfunctory smattering of glossy brochures on the island and a free road map. For more practical information about any big events on while you're in town, you'll need to rely on flyers, newspaper and radio ads and word of mouth.

Safety and harassment

On the whole St John's is an extremely safe city and, during the daytime at least, you'll be undisturbed wandering around. There are a few hustlers who zero in on obvious foreigners – asking you to buy something or begging for change – but they are rarely persistent or threatening. At night most of the city is unlit and there is a little more of a sense of menace, particularly around the very poor areas to the south (though you'll never have any reason to venture there). Stick to the centre, where you'll find the restaurants and bars, and you're highly unlikely to encounter any hassle.

For details of accommodation in St John's, see p.90; for eating and drinking see p.103.

The city

The small centre of **St John's** is easily explored on foot, and you should certainly make your way to **Redcliffe Quay** – where the waterfront and its colonial buildings have been attractively restored – as well as the tiny **National Museum**, which offers a well-presented run-down on the country's history and culture. If you've got time, take a stroll through some of the old streets, and check out the city's twin-towered **cathedral** perched on top of Newgate Street. **Redcliffe Quay** and nearby **Heritage Quay** are the best places to eat, drink and shop for souvenirs, though you'll probably want to avoid them if the cruise-ships are in, when the steel drums come out to play "Hot, Hot, Hot" and the area almost disappears beneath a scrum of duty-free shoppers.

Some history

Although it is now by far Antigua's biggest town, St John's was not the first major settlement on the island, a distinction that went to Falmouth on the south coast (see p.59). The first reference to St John's was made in the 1660s,

THE CITY

when the colonists decided to build a town that could take full advantage of the excellent natural harbour. Though St John's suffered almost immediate **invasion** by the French, who sailed in and destroyed the fledgling town in 1668, it quickly grew into a prosperous city which, with its great location at the northeastern corner of the Caribbean – making it one of the first islands to be reached by ships sailing from Europe – became the area's leading business centre.

The city's major buildings were determined by colonial Antigua's two chief concerns – **trade** and **security**. Warehouses were erected by the quays to store sugar and molasses prior to export and barracoons were built to hold the imported slaves, while forts were built at strategic points around the harbour to deter further invasion. Natural disasters and disease were regular visitors: in particular, a yellow fever epidemic in 1793 wiped out many of the inhabitants, while a devastating fire in 1841 gutted most of the city's old buildings.

As the nineteenth century progressed, the declining fortunes of sugar (see p.137) meant that St John's began to lose much of its former lustre and – though still the capital city – it gradually became something of a provincial backwater. However, the tourist boom of the last few decades has prompted a concerted effort to spruce the place up and, with the quay area in particular now well-restored, it is still possible to catch a whiff of the city's glory days.

AROUND REDCLIFFE QUAY

Map 3, D4.

Spread over several acres by the waterside, **Redcliffe Quay** is probably the best place to start your tour of the city. Named in honour of the church of St Mary Redcliffe in the English port city of Bristol, this is one of the oldest parts of St John's, and incorporates many old warehouses – now attractively restored as small boutiques, restaurants and bars – and a wooden boardwalk that runs alongside the water. There's not a huge amount to see, but it's a pleasant place to wander and soak up some of the city's history.

Many of the warehouses once held supplies for the British navy and local merchant ships that traded between Antigua and the mother country during the eighteenth century – barrels of sugar and rum, lumber for ship repairs, cotton and sheepskins – while the area behind the quay held a number of barracoons, compounds where slaves were held after they arrived on the island and before they were sent off to the plantations or shipped on to other Caribbean islands. **Coates Cottage** on Nevis Street, an art gallery undergoing restoration work at the time of writing, is built on the site of one such barracoon, and you can wander through to the small walled courtyard where the slaves were held. The adjacent and much-restored bright pink wooden building was once a **bargaining house**, where auctions were held and slaves sold off to local estate-owners.

Back at the front of the quay, a short stroll north takes you up to **Heritage Quay** at the foot of High Street. This modern concrete quay is given over to cruise-ship arrivals and dozens of duty free shops designed to catch their tourist dollars, along with a few roadside stalls where local vendors flog T-shirts and distinctive Haitian art. Unless you're shopping or heading to the King's Casino (see p.116), there's no reason to stop except for a quick look at the **cenotaph** – a memorial to Antiguans who died during World War I – a **monument to V.C. Bird** – first prime minister of the independent country – and the **Westerby Memorial**, which commemorates a Moravian missionary dedicated to helping Antiguans in the decades after emancipation from slavery in 1834.

AROUND REDCLIFFE QUAY

The Rec

Modest and unassuming as it looks, the **Antigua Recreation Ground** is one of the finest cricket pitches in the Caribbean. Blessed by low rainfall and year-round sun, and with its outfield and wicket lovingly tended by trusted inmates from the nearby prison, it looks at quiet times like any cricket pitch in England or Australia. Don't believe it for a moment. On match days, while the rest of the island comes to a standstill, the ground is transformed into a cacophonous whirligig, with music belting from the stands, hordes of vendors flogging jerk chicken and Red Stripe, men on stilts, women in wigs and the ever-present and iconic Gravy stalking around in high heels, national costume or a spangly red dress as the mood takes him.

If you've got any sense of adventure, head for Chickie's Double Decker stand at the north end of the ground. With his banks of huge speakers tied to the railings, the eponymous deejay blasts players and fans alike with the songs of local calypsonians, and everyone barks along to the chorus of "Who let the dog out?" Bumping and grinding away, more intent on the beer and the chat-up lines than the cricket, the happy spectators will be there long after stumps have been drawn and the players have retired to the pavilion.

LONG STREET AND AROUND

One block north of the tourist office, Long Street runs east as far as the **Antigua Recreation Ground**, the country's main cricket venue and the home to most of the action during the ten-day Carnival each July and August (see p.117). The street has many of St John's finest old buildings, including a couple of fabulously colourful liquor stores, still in operation more than a century since first opening.

The National Museum

Map 3, E2. Mon–Fri 8.30am–4pm; Sat 10am–2pm; free.

Housed in a 1747 Neoclassical courthouse on the corner of Long and Market streets, the **National Museum of Antigua and Barbuda** occupies just one room, but it's indisputably worth 45 minutes of your time while you're exploring the capital – you can almost feel the enthusiasm with which the collection has been assembled and displayed. The exhibits start by showing off the islands' early geological history, backed up by fossils and coral skeletons, and move on to more extensive coverage of its first, Amerindian inhabitants. Jewellery, primitive tools, pottery shards and religious figures used by these early settlers have been found at sites across Antigua and Barbuda and are well laid out, with brief descriptions of their significance.

Continuing chronologically, there are brief displays on Columbus, the European invasion, and sugar production – the country's raison d'etre from the mid-seventeenth century. An interesting 1750 map of Antigua shows the plantations, as well as all the reefs that threatened shipping around the island. There is also an unusual exhibit on the emancipation of the slaves and the resulting patterns of settlement. At emancipation in 1834 there were only four towns on Antigua, with almost all the ex-slaves living on the sugar estates; the planters usually refused to sell them land, since they wanted to keep them tied to the plantations. The exhibit shows how – with the assistance of missionaries or by sheer determination – the former slaves were able to set themselves up in "free villages" across the island.

For more on Antigua's early Ameridian population, see History, p.133.

THE NATIONAL MUSEUM |

Vivi

One of the museum's most prized exhibits is the cricket bat with which, in 1986, Antiguan **Viv Richards** scored the fastest ever test match century, taking just 56 balls to score 100 runs against England on his home turf. It's hard to over-estimate the importance of Vivi (as he's known locally) to the development of the country's self-confidence in the years immediately before and after independence in 1981. For this tiny island to have produced a man rated by many as the finest batsman of his generation was an enormous boost to its self-esteem. Richards wasn't the first Antiguan to play for the West Indies cricket team – fast bowler Andy Roberts won that honour a few months earlier – but his spectacular hitting and imperious manner endeared him to a generation of cricket-watchers world-wide. Now retired, Richards has eschewed the political career many expected, but the street where he was born in St John's now bears his name and – as a "goodwill ambassador" – he remains one of Antigua's most precious living assets.

Elsewhere, there are displays on the island of Barbuda – which might whet your appetite for a visit (see p.76) – and the tiny uninhabited rock of Redonda (see p.84). There's also an example of the ancient board game warri or mancala, brought by slaves from Africa's Gold Coast, and, rather bizarrely, a rhinoceros skull from Rwanda. Once you've finished your tour, take a peek in the small gift shop, where you can pick up pottery, reproduction maps of the islands, postcards and books.

Directly behind the museum, the **police station** – formerly the city's arsenal – is one of the oldest surviving buildings in the city. The long stone building beside it, also part of the police station, was the island's first jail, while the iron railings in the station's courtyard are made from the barrels and bayonets of nineteenth-century muskets.

ST JOHN'S CATHEDRAL

Map 3, F2. Daily 9am–5pm; free

East of here, and towering over the city at the far end of Newgate Street, the imposing twin towers of the **Cathedral Church of St John the Divine** are the capital's dominant landmark. A simple wooden church was first built on this hilltop site in 1681 and, after heavy destruction was wrought by a number of earthquakes and hurricanes, the present cathedral was put up in 1847.

From the outside, the grey stone Neo-Baroque building is not particularly prepossessing – squat and bulky with the two towers capped by slightly awkward cupolas. More attractively, the airy interior of the cathedral is almost entirely encased in dark pine, designed to hold the building together in the event of earthquake or hurricane, and the walls are dotted with marble tablets commemorating distinguished figures from the island's history, some of them rescued from the wreck of earlier churches here and incorporated into the new cathedral. In the grounds of the cathedral, the whitewashed and equally baroque **lead figures** on the south gate – taken from a French ship near Martinique in the 1750s during the Seven Years' War between France and Britain – represent St John the Baptist and St John the Divine, draped in flowing robes.

THE MARKET

Map 3, E6. Mon–Sat from around 6am.

One other colourful site worth checking out is the public **market** at the south end of Market Street, a road once known as Scotch Row in honour of the traders – many of them early Scottish immigrants who fled to the West Indies to escape the tyranny of seventeenth- and eighteenth-century English landowners – who once lined it with their shops selling sugar, indigo, coffee, tobacco and rum. Today it remains an important shopping thoroughfare, with the public market the place to head to for exotic fruit, vegetables and fish. As you'd expect, it's a lively, bustling place with a fine variety of food, particularly on Friday and Saturday – head down and pick up some sapodillas, papayas and mangoes for great snacking.

Fort Bay

A short drive or taxi-ride from town, heading north from St John's on Fort Road, a left turn at the *Barrymore Hotel* takes you out to the capital city's most popular beach and some of the best-preserved **military ruins** on the island. The road winds its way around to the coast at **Fort Bay**, where a long, wide strand of grainy white sand – packed with city dwellers at weekends and holidays – offers the nearest quality beach to town. At its northern end, you can hire beach chairs from Miller's – a good place, too, to pick up a drink – and there's a vendors' mall nearby if you want to hunt for souvenirs.

At the other end of the strip, a host of food and drink stalls open up at busy times when a crowd descends from town, transforming the place into a lively outdoor venue, with music blaring, fish frying and plenty of frolicking on the beach. If you want to swim, there's a protected, marked area at the top of the beach; elsewhere, the water is normally fine but you'll need to watch out for occasional undercurrents.

FORT JAMES

Map 2, C7. Always open; free.

Continue south along the coast to eighteenth-century **Fort James**, built up above the cliffs that overlook the entrance to St John's harbour. You can walk or drive around to the south side of the fort, where the main gate is still in place. Together with Fort Barrington, on the opposite side of the channel (see p.75) and St John's Fort on Rat Island – still visible down the channel – this fort was designed to deter any ships from attacking the capital, which had been sacked by French raiders in 1668. Earthworks were first raised in the 1680s, though the bulk of the fort was put up in 1739, when the long enclosing wall was added. The place never fired a shot in anger, although its guns undoubtedly intimidated visiting vessels into paying the eighteen shillings levied in the eighteenth century to the fort's captain.

Today, the fort is in pretty good shape, and offers plenty of atmosphere: unkempt, often windswept and providing great views across the channel and back down to St John's harbour. Ten rusting British cannons from the early 1800s point out to sea and down the channel, their threat long gone but still a dramatic symbol of their era. Elsewhere, the old powder magazine is still intact, though leaning precariously, and the stone buildings on the fort's upper level – the oldest part of the structure, dating from 1705 – include the master gunner's house, the canteen and the barracks. At the northern tip of the fort, *Russell's* is a good place to grab a drink and a snack after you've explored.

Shopping

St John's is a reasonable target for **shoppers** and, given its limited size, there's a surprising amount of choice. By the water, Heritage Quay has a broad range of **duty-free stores** – including international chains like Body Shop and Benetton – selling designer clothes, jewellery and liquor. Nearby Redcliffe Quay has more designer clothes stores while, down a notch in quality, the adjoining streets are crowded with stalls offering T-shirts, Haitian paintings and various **souvenir** knick-knacks.

For **food**, there's the enormous Bryson's supermarket on Long Street (Mon–Sat 8am–9pm, Sun 9am–4pm), and a range of tropical fruit, vegetables and fish at the market downtown. There's not much else around the city, although the beautiful old **liquor** stores on Long Street stock Antigua's Cavalier and English Harbour rums as well as other, better Caribbean rums, including Barbados's Mount Gay Extra Old and Haiti's Barbancourt Reserve.

The American mall-style Woods Centre, five minutes' drive north of town, is mainly targeted at Antiguan shoppers, and oozes local affluence. You'll find the island's best-stocked **supermarket**, Epicurean (daily 8am–10pm), though prices are pretty hefty; its finest **bookshop**, First Edition (Mon–Sat 9am–9pm); as well as banks, fast food outlets, a post office, a gym and plenty more. A courtesy bus runs to the centre from the west bus station in St John's, near the market.

From Runaway Bay to Half Moon Bay

Heading north of St John's, **Runaway Bay** and adjoining **Dickenson Bay** constitute the island's main tourist strip, with a couple of excellent beaches, a host of top-notch hotels and restaurants and plenty of action. Continuing clockwise round the island brings you to its Atlantic side, where the jagged coastline offers plenty of inlets, bays and swamps but, with a couple of noteworthy exceptions, rather less impressive beaches. Tourist facilities on this side of the island are much less developed, but there are several places of interest. **Betty's Hope** is a restored sugar plantation; **Parham**, the island's first port, has a lovely old church; **Devil's Bridge** offers one of the most dramatic landscapes on the island; and at picturesque **Half Moon Bay** you can scramble along a vertiginous cliff-top path above the pounding Atlantic.

RUNAWAY BAY AND DICKENSON BAY

A few kilometres north of St John's, a series of attractive white sand beaches run around the island's northwest coast.

Most of the tourist development has happened along Runaway Bay and Dickenson Bay, where the gleaming beaches slope gently down into the turquoise sea, offering calm swimming and, at the northern end of Dickenson Bay, a host of watersports. **Runaway Bay** is the quieter of the two and, because there are fewer hotels to tidy up their "patch", is strewn with more seaweed and rocks. It's still a great place to wander in the gentle surf, though at the northern end much of the beach was eroded by heavy swells in late 1996.

Just beyond here, grassy **Corbison Point** pokes out into the sea, dividing the bay from Dickenson Bay. A stone igloo-shaped powder store is the sole remnant of an eighteenth-century British **fort** that once stood here, and the cliff has also revealed Amerindian potsherds and evidence that more ancient island-dwellers exploited flint in the area for their tools. Heading north of the point, you'll have to detour briefly onto the road to bypass the marina at the *Marina Bay Hotel*, before returning to the beach.

Trapped between two imposing sandstone bluffs, **Dickenson Bay** is fringed by another wide, white sandy beach, which stretches for almost a mile between Corbison Point and the more thickly vegetated woodland of Weatherills Hill at its northern end. It's a lovely bay, shelving gently into the sea and with a protected swimming zone dividing swimmers from the jet-skiers, windsurfers, water-skiers and parasailers who frolic offshore. The northern half of the beach fronts some of the largest of Antigua's hotels, including the *Rex Halcyon Cove*, whose pier juts out into the sea and offers dining above the ocean, and *Sandals Antigua*, with its striking yellow pavilions. As a result, particularly in high season, the area can get pretty busy, with a string of bars, hair-braiders and T-shirt sellers doing a brisk trade, but it's still an easygoing place, with minimal hassle.

An old clapboard house in St John's

The road into St John's from English Harbour

Rum shop in Jennings

The ruined eighteenth-century boathouse at English Harbour

Devil's Bridge, on the north coast of Antigua

Fabric shop in St John's

The Admiral's House at Nelson's Dockyard

Military ruins from the British colonial era on Shirley Heights

Hurricane Luis

In September 1995 **Hurricane Luis** pulverized Antigua. Sweeping ashore near the Half Moon Hotel on the east coast it caused extensive damage everywhere, ripping up hotels, houses and tin shacks, laying waste fields of crops and leaving two people dead and thousands homeless. Aid poured into the island and, in many parts (particularly the main tourist areas), life returned to normal remarkably quickly. But, particularly in the east and around Runaway Bay, it has taken a lot longer to repair the damage, and you'll find plenty of evidence of the destruction as you explore.

Divided by the coast road from Runaway Bay and the southern end of Dickenson Bay, **McKinnon's Salt Pond** is an extensive area of brackish water edged by mangroves and a good place for bird-spotting. More than 25 species of water birds have been recorded here, most noticeably the big flocks of sandpipers which wheel above the pond, as well as terns and plovers which nest on the sand and red-footed herons which breed in the mangroves. Seabirds can also be seen at either end of the beach, swooping gracefully around the sandstone bluffs; watch out in particular for the pelicans, showing off their clumsy but spectacular technique of divebombing for fish.

For details of accommodation in Runaway Bay and Dickenson Bay, see p.92; for eating and drinking see p.108.

HURRICANE LUIS

ISLAND ARTS

Map 2, E1. Mon–Sat 9am–5pm.

There are few points of interest worth stopping off for on the northeast coast, but Nick Maley's **Island Arts Gallery** in Hodges Bay is certainly one of them. Maley, originally a film make-up artist who worked on movies like *Star Wars* and *Krull*, is a British painter who has worked on Antigua for over a decade and shown his striking and original works at exhibitions across the Caribbean and North America. Maley's small gallery and studio – resonating to the squawks of the parrots he and his wife breed in their lush garden – are crammed with his paintings and prints, as well as those of Antiguan, Haitian and other West Indian artists. Though the artists are mostly little-known outside their home islands, there is plenty of exuberant colour and some captivating local portraits (look for Maley's "Illustration of a Girl"), beside the more predictable land and seascapes. The gallery is signposted up a side street, beside the hurricane-battered *Hodges Bay Hotel*, off the main road that skirts the northeast coast.

FITCHES CREEK BAY AND PARHAM

Map 2, E3 and D3.

East of the airport, a rocky road loops round **Fitches Creek Bay**, a desolate inlet with no beaches of note, dotted with brackish mangrove swamps; birdwatchers can look out for herons, egrets and whistling ducks among the multitude of local species. **St George's Parish Church**, first built in 1687 – though hurricane and earthquake damage have long since taken their toll – overlooks the bay. At the time of writing the place has been gutted and a new roof is being raised, but the ancient, weathered brick walls and crumbling tombs facing out to sea still lend it a strong sense of history.

The road continues around the bay to **PARHAM**. First settled in the seventeenth century, it is one of the oldest inhabited towns on the island. By far the most impressive building in town is the octagonal **St Peter's Parish Church**, considered unique in the Caribbean. A wooden church was first erected here in 1711, although the present structure mostly dates from 1840. The inside is spacious and airy, with tall windows capped with brick arches and a handful of marble commemorative tablets to nineteenth-century local notables. The unusual wooden ribbed ceiling is especially striking; the design – like an upturned ship's hull – has delightful simplicity.

Outside, the cemetery tumbles down the hill towards **Parham Harbour**, Antigua's first port. Protected from the Atlantic waves by offshore islands, this fine natural anchorage was busy with oceangoing ships for more than two centuries until sugar exports slumped in the 1920s. Now it shelters yachts and small fishing vessels – there's a small jetty at the eastern end of town but few other port facilities to testify to its heyday.

BETTY'S HOPE

Map 2, D4. Tues–Sat 10am–4pm; EC$6.

From Parham, the road leads south and then east at the petrol station towards the partly restored **Betty's Hope**, the island's very first sugar estate. Built in 1650, the place was owned by the Codrington family for nearly two centuries until the end of World War II; by that time its lack of profitability had brought it to the edge of the closure, which followed soon after. Although parts of the estate still lie in ruins, one of the windmills has been restored to working condition, and a small and interesting museum at the visitor centre tells the history of sugar on Antigua and explains the development and restoration of the estate.

DEVIL'S BRIDGE AND LONG BAY

Map 2, B4.

East of Betty's Hope, the landscape becomes more prairie-like, with cattle roaming over the gently rolling hills. On your left, the otherwise unremarkable **St Stephen's Anglican Church** has recently been rebuilt to a curious design, with the pulpit in the centre and the pews on each side; outside, the crumbling tombs in the flower-strewn cemetery suggest that the place has been a religious site for several centuries.

Approaching Long Bay, a road signposted off to the right takes you out to **Devil's Bridge**, on a rocky outcrop edged by patches of grassy land, tall century plants and sunbathing cattle. Wander round the promontory to the "bridge", a narrow piece of rock whose underside has been washed away by thousands of years of relentless surf action. The hot, windswept spot offers some of the most fetching views on the island, back across a quiet cove to the new *Mango Bay Hotel* and out across the lashing ocean and dark reefs to a series of small islands just offshore. En route back to the main road, a dirt track on your right after 400 metres leads down to a tiny but gorgeous bay – the perfect venue for a picnic. The place plays occasional host to some local parties, and can get rather litter-strewn, but the turquoise sea is exceptionally inviting and the normally empty strip of white beach a great place to chill out.

At the end of the main road, **Long Bay** is home to a couple of rather exclusive all-inclusives, which doesn't stop you from getting access to a great, wide bay, enormously popular with local schoolkids, who can often be found splashing around or playing cricket at one end of the beach. The lengthy spread of white sand is protected by an extensive reef a few hundred metres offshore – bring your snorkelling gear – and there's a great little beach bar for shelter and refreshment when you've had enough sun.

The hike along Soldier Point

There's an excellent 45-minute **hike** along **Soldier Point**, the headland at the southern end of the bay, just beyond the hotel. Where the beach ends you can clamber up onto the rocks and a trail – marked by splashes of blue paint along its entire length – cuts left along the edge of the cliff. It's a moderately tough climb, with a bit of a scramble required in places, but well worth it for some fine views out to sea and over the bay, dramatic scenery carved by the waves and – apart from butterflies and seabirds – a sense of splendid isolation. Don't go barefoot – the rocks are sharp in places and there are plenty of thorns around.

HALF MOON BAY

Map 2, B5.

One of the prettiest spots on Antigua, **Half Moon Bay** has a kilometre-long semicircle of white sand beach partially enclosing a deep blue bay, where the Atlantic surf normally offers top-class body-surfing opportunities. The isolation of this side of the island means that the beach is often pretty empty, especially since the closure, after Hurricane Luis, of the expensive hotel at its southern end. However, there is a parking lot beside the beach and a shack selling drinks and snacks.

HALF MOON BAY

Falmouth and English Harbour

An essential stop on any visit to Antigua, the picturesque area around **Falmouth** and **English Harbour** on the island's south coast holds some of the most important and interesting historical remains in the Caribbean and is now the regions's leading yachting centre. The chief attraction is the eighteenth-century **Nelson's Dockyard**, which was the key facility for the British navy that once ruled the waves in the area; today it's a living museum where the numerous visiting yachts are still cleaned, supplied and chartered, with several ruined forts nearby as well as an abundance of attractive colonial buildings on the waterfront, several now converted into hotels and restaurants.

Across the harbour from the dockyard, there is further evidence of the colonial past at **Shirley Heights**, where more ruined forts, gun batteries and an old cemetery hold a commanding position over the water. It's a dramatic place whose rather forlorn air is shattered on Sunday evenings when steel and reggae bands lend sound to a lively (if somewhat over-touristed) barbecue party.

> **For details of accommodation in Falmouth and English Harbour, see p.96; for eating and drinking see p.111.**

The area also has a handful of far less visited spots that repay a trip, including the massive military complex at **Great Fort George**, high in the hills above **Falmouth**, and the wonderful **Rendezvous Bay** – outstanding in an area with a paucity of good beaches – a boat ride or less than an hour's hike from Falmouth.

Getting there and getting around

A car is invaluable for touring around this area of the south coast. There are frequent **buses** between St John's and English Harbour, handy if you just want to explore Nelson's Dockyard, but to get up to Shirley Heights you'll certainly need your own transport.

Falmouth and around

The main road south from St John's, cutting through the very centre of Antigua, first hits the coast at **Falmouth Harbour**. This large and beautiful natural harbour has been used as a safe anchorage since the days of the earliest colonists, and the town which sprang up beside it was the first major settlement on the island. Today, though the harbour is still often busy with yachts, Falmouth itself is a quiet place, most of the activity in the area having moved west to **English Harbour**, divided from Falmouth Harbour by a small peninsula known as the **Middle Ground**.

The hike to Rendezvous Bay

Although there is no beach of particular note in Falmouth, you can make a great hike from just west of town to **Rendezvous Bay,** the most idyllic and one of the quietest beaches on Antigua. Heading out of town, turn left on Farrell Avenue and follow the road round past the colourful Rainbow School onto a dirt track edged with banana groves. Take a right at the first intersection, past the Spring Hill Riding Club, then, at the fork, go left up a hill that soon becomes paved. There's a big, white house at the top of the hill; park near it and follow the track that veers off to the left. If you don't have a car, it'll take you around 25 minutes to reach this point from the top of Farrell Avenue.

The track climbs briefly between Cherry Hill and Sugar Loaf Hill, allowing great views back over Falmouth Harbour, then drops down through the scrubby bush, with sea grape and acacia trees on either side. After 25 minutes you'll reach a rocky bay, strewn with conch shells, and a further 10-minute wander along the beach brings you to Rendezvous Bay, an aquamarine sea with a curve of fine white sand backed by coconut palms and dotted with driftwood. It's a gorgeous place to swim – the comparatively remote location means that there is rarely anyone else here, although the occasional **boat trip** makes its way across from Falmouth to use a thatched barbecue hut recently built on the beach and offering welcome shade. Bring some water, a picnic, a book and some snorkelling gear, and you could easily spend half a day here.

There's little in town to stop for, but you may want to pay a brief visit to **St Paul's Church**, right alongside the main road. The original wooden church (long since destroyed by a hurricane) was the island's first, dating from

RENDEZVOUS BAY

the 1660s. Its modern successor is rarely open, but among the cracked eighteenth-century tombstones that cover the east side of the extensive graveyard is that of James Pitt, brother of the British prime minister, who died in English Harbour in 1780.

GREAT FORT GEORGE

Map 5, C2.

High above Falmouth, and offering terrific panoramic views over the harbour and surrounding countryside, are the ruins of **Great George Fort** (also known as Monk's Hill), one of Antigua's oldest defences. During the late seventeenth century, England was at war with France, whose navy captured the nearby island of St Kitts in 1686. To repel any invaders from Antigua, the English decided to build a large fort on the hills behind the island's main town, together with housing and water cisterns to provide a secure retreat for Antigua's tiny population.

Though the French never in fact invaded, the fort was eventually completed in 1705, with dozens of cannon pointing in all directions. Barracks and gunpowder stores were added during the following century. With its seemingly impregnable position, Great George is likely to have been an important factor in deterring possible invasion. By the mid-nineteenth century, when any threat of invasion had receded, the fort was employed as a signal station, using flags to report on the movement of ships in and around Falmouth harbour.

**For more on the colonial history
of Antigua, see p.133.**

Today, the fort is in a very ruinous state, but it's well worth the effort to get to for the fabulous views and – as there's

GREAT FORT GEORGE

rarely anyone there – a quiet but evocative sense of the island's past. Much of the enormous stone perimeter wall is intact while, inside the main gate and to the right, the west gunpowder magazine (built in 1731) has been well restored. It's fun to wander around the rest of the extensive scrub-covered ruins and see if you can identify which part was living quarters and which part military establishment.

To get to the fort you'll need a four-wheel drive vehicle or a 30-minute hike. A precipitous but passable track leads up from the village of Cobbs Cross, east of Falmouth; alternatively, from Liberta (north of Falmouth) take the inland road to Table Hill Gordon, from where another track winds up to the fort.

English Harbour and around

The road east from Falmouth leads to Cobb's Cross, where a right turn takes you down to the small village of **ENGLISH HARBOUR**, which today consists of little more than a handful of homes, shops and restaurants. Another right turn leads down to **Nelson's Dockyard** and the Middle Ground peninsula that divides Falmouth Harbour from English Harbour; alternatively, head left for the road that climbs up into the hills to the military ruins at **Shirley Heights**.

NELSON'S DOCKYARD

Map 5, E5. Daily 8am–6pm; EC$6.50.
One of Antigua's definite highlights, the eighteenth-century **Nelson's Dockyard** is the only surviving Georgian dockyard

"This infernal hole"

The link between British Admiral **Horatio Nelson** and the dockyard named in his honour is somewhat tenuous. From 1784 to 1787, Nelson (aged 26 at the start of his tour of duty) commanded the Northern Division of the Leeward Island Station, based in English Harbour. There is little suggestion that he enjoyed his posting, indeed he referred to Antigua in correspondence as "a vile spot" and "this infernal hole". No doubt he was itching to engage the French in battle – something that he was to achieve (to his cost) some 20 years later – rather than sitting around swatting mosquitos and chasing pirates. Nonetheless, after restoration in the 1950s the Antigua tourist board evidently decided a famous title was needed to help market the place, and so the name Nelson's Dockyard was born.

in the world, and a delightful place to wander in. Adjacent to a fine natural harbour, the place developed primarily as a careening station – a place where British ships were brought to have the barnacles scraped from their bottoms and generally put back into shape. It provided a crucial function for the military, providing them with a local base to repair, water and supply the navy that patrolled the West Indies and protected Britain's prized colonies against enemy incursion.

The dockyard was begun in 1743, and most of the present buildings date from between 1785 and 1792, many of them – like the atmospheric *Admiral's Inn* hotel – built from the ballast of bricks and stones brought to the island by British trading ships, who sailed "empty" from home en route to loading up with sugar and rum.

During the nineteenth century, however, the advent of steam-powered ships, which needed less attention, coincided

NELSON'S DOCKYARD

with a decline in British interest in the region, and the dockyard fell into disuse, finally closing in 1889. Over the next 60 years the buildings took a battering from hurricanes and earthquakes, but the 1950s saw a major restoration project, and in 1961 the dockyard was officially re-opened as both a working harbour and a tourist attraction.

The sights

The main road ends at an extensive parking area, from where the entrance to the dockyard – where you can pick up an information sheet on the area – takes you past the local post office, a bank and a large **covered market**, where vendors compete languidly for custom for their T-shirts and other local souvenirs.

Entering the lane beyond this mini-commercial zone, the first building on your left is the **Admiral's Inn**, built in 1788 and originally used as a store for pitch, lead and turpentine, with offices for the dockyard's engineers upstairs. Today the place acts as a hotel and restaurant, and is one of the most atmospheric spots on the south coast. Adjoining the hotel, a dozen thick, capped **stone pillars** – looking like the relics of an ancient Greek temple – are all that remain of a large boathouse, where ships were pulled in along a narrow channel to have their sails repaired in the sail-loft on the upper floor.

From the hotel, a lane leads down to the harbour, passing various restored colonial buildings, including the remains of a guardhouse, a blacksmith's workshop and an old canvas and clothing store that provided supplies for the ships. On your right is a 200-year-old sandbox tree and, just beyond it, the Admiral's House (a local residence that never actually housed an admiral) which was built in 1855 and today serves as the dockyard's museum. The museum (daily 8am–6pm; free) is worth a quick tour for its small but diverse collection that focuses principally on the island's shipping tradition, with models and photographs of old schooners and battleships, and cups and records celebrating the various races held during the annual Sailing Week, when English Harbour almost disappears under a tide of visiting yachts, their owners and crews.

For more information on Sailing Week at English Harbour, see p.126.

Just beyond the museum, the bougainvillea-festooned **Copper and Lumber Store** now serves as an elegant hotel and restaurant; beyond that are the officers' quarters – one of the most striking buildings in the dockyard, with a graceful double-staircase sweeping up to a long, arcaded verandah. Ships' officers lived here during the hurricane season, when most of the fleet put into English Harbour for protection. The building sits on a huge water cistern of 12 separate tanks, with a capacity for 240,000 gallons of water, and today provides space for an art gallery, boutique, bar and other stores, while the downstairs offices house the immigration and customs authorities.

Across from the building, three black and white **capstans** – formerly enclosed in a capstan house – have been thoroughly restored. These were used in the careening of ships; each mast was roped to a capstan, which was then rotated to turn the ship on its side. Behind the capstan and surrounded by iron railings is an old sundial.

There are a couple of good dive operators based at Nelson's Dockyard – see p.121.

NELSON'S DOCKYARD

Walking on the Middle Ground

For some rather more strenuous hiking, a right turn just before you reach Fort Berkeley leads up a poorly-defined track to the peninsula known as the **Middle Ground**, where more military ruins dot the landscape. It's a stiff clamber to the top of the hill, where a circular base is all that remains of the one-gun Keane battery that stood here until the early nineteenth century, but you get a clear picture of the strategic importance of the Middle Ground for defending both Falmouth Harbour to the west and English Harbour to the east.

Continuing the hike on the other side of the hill leads down and then up to the remains of **Fort Cuyler**, where more gun emplacements and crumbling barracks walls are further testimony to the military domination of the area. You'll need all your tracking skills to keep to the paths around here – goats and the occasional goatherd are the only users of the old soldiers' tracks these days, and there is a fair amount of prickly cactus and thorn bush to contend with – but the hike offers spectacular views over the harbours and the ocean, as well as the desert-like landscape.

FORT BERKELEY

Map 5, F6.

The narrow path that leads from behind the copper and lumber store to **Fort Berkeley** is easily overlooked, but a stroll around these dramatic military ruins should be an integral part of your visit. Built onto a narrow spit of land that commands the entrance to English Harbour, the fort was the harbour's earliest defensive point and retains essentially the same shape today that it had in 1745.

The path leads down to the water's edge; go around the jetty and some steps take you up to a trail leading to the fort, ten minutes' walk away out on to the headland. On your right as you approach, above the craggy wave-swept rocks, cannons once lined most of the wall facing out to sea, with the main body of the fort at the far end of the walkway comprising sentry boxes, a recently restored guardhouse and a gunpowder magazine or store. A handful of early nineteenth-century Scottish cannons are still dotted around the ruined fort, and the place offers spectacular views out to sea and back across the sand-fringed harbour.

In 1750, to deter surprise attacks by small boats, a chain was stretched across the mouth of the harbour between Fort Berkeley and its sister fort, Fort Charlotte; today, the chain is long gone and little more than rubble remains of Charlotte, destroyed by the same 1843 earthquake that demolished much of the original wall of Fort Berkeley.

SHIRLEY HEIGHTS

Map 5, G6.
Spread over an extensive area of the hills to the east of English Harbour, numerous ruined military buildings offer further evidence of the strategic importance of this part of southern Antigua. Collectively known as **Shirley Heights** (although technically this is only the name for the area around Fort Shirley), it's an interesting area to explore, with a couple of hiking opportunities for the adventurous who want to escape the crowd completely.

Some history

The area of Shirley Heights is named after General Sir Thomas Shirley, governor of the Leeward Islands based in Antigua from 1781 to 1791. At a time when British

Caribbean possessions were fast falling to the French – Dominica in 1778, St Vincent and Grenada in 1779 – and with British forces in America surrendering in 1781, Shirley insisted on massive fortification of Antigua to protect the naval dockyard. Building continued steadily for the next decade and, although the threat diminished after the French were finally defeated in 1815, the military complex was manned until 1854, since when it has been steadily eroded by a succession of hurricanes and earthquakes.

The sights

Follow the road uphill from the tiny village of English Harbour, ignoring the left-hand turn-offs to a couple of rather pricey hotels and restaurants that line the coast, and you'll pass the **Dow Hill Interpretation Centre** (daily 9am–5pm; EC$10) which, frankly, has virtually nothing to do with the history of the area and is pretty missable. Outside you'll find the scant remains of the **Dow's Hill fort**; indoors, there's a great collection of local shells and a 15-minute "multimedia" exhibition, with an adult voice answering a child's questions about the country's history from the Stone Age to the present.

Beyond the centre, the road runs along the top of a ridge before dividing where a large cannon has been upended in the centre of the road. Fork left for the cliff known as **Cape Shirley**, where you'll find a collection of ruined stone buildings – including barracks, officers' quarters and an arms storeroom – known collectively as the **Blockhouse**. On the eastern side a wide gun platform, sprinkled with old iron cannons during restoration work, looks downhill to **Indian Creek** (see box on p.70), beyond that to the **Standfast Point** peninsula and Eric Clapton's enormous house and gatehouse, and beyond that over the vast sweep of Willoughby Bay. Every year, stories leak out of Clapton and friends like Elton John and Keith Richard turning up for a jam at one of the island's nightclubs.

If you take the right-hand fork at the half-buried cannon, the road will lead you up to the further ruins of Fort Shirley. On the right as you approach are the still grandly arcaded though now roofless officers' quarters, overgrown with grass and grazed by the ubiquitous goats; opposite, across a bare patch of ground, are the ruins of the military hospital and, in a small valley just below the surgeon's quarters, the **military cemetery** with its barely legible tombstones dating mostly from the 1850s and reflecting the prevalence of disease – particularly yellow fever – and an obelisk commemorating the men of the Dorset regiment who died in service during the 1840s.

The road ends at the fort itself, where a restored guardhouse now serves as an excellent little bar and restaurant. Beyond the guardhouse, the courtyard of the **Lookout** – where once a battery of cannons pointed out across the sea – now sees a battery of cameras snapping up the fabulous views over English Harbour, particularly on Sundays when the tourists descend in droves for the reggae and steel bands.

For more information on live music at the Lookout, see p.119.

Around Mamora Bay

Map 5, D6.

From Cobbs Cross, avoiding the right turn to English Harbour, the road runs east towards a couple of quiet bays, including tiny Mamora Bay and the huge curve of Willoughby Bay. It's an attractive drive, though there is little specific to see; Mamora Bay is now dominated by the exclusive *St James Club* and the road past Willoughby Bay winds up through pineapple fields towards the old Betty's Hope sugar plantation (see p.55) and the island's east coast.

A hike to Indian Creek

From the blockhouse it's a short but steep downhill **hike** down to the bluff which overlooks **Indian Creek** where, scattered along the shoreline, some of the island's most important Amerindian finds have been made. The hike passes down through dense scrubby grassland tended by goats and covered in cacti, particularly the rather phallic red and green Turk's head cacti. At the bottom of the hill there's a small, sheltered but rocky beach, not great for swimming, while the path continues up through a wood of cracked acacia trees and onto the deserted bluff, which offers grand views over the creek and, further east, over Mamora Bay and Willoughby Bay.

The West Coast

Antigua's **west coast** is dominated by tourism, with large hotels dotted at regular intervals between the little fishing village of **Old Road** in the south and the capital, St John's. Two features dominate the area: a series of lovely beaches, with **Darkwood** probably the pick of the bunch for swimming, snorkelling and beachcombing, and a glowering range of hills known as the **Shekerley Mountains** in the southwest, offering the chance for a climb and some panoramic views. The lush and thickly wooded **Fig Tree Hill** on the edge of the range is as scenic a spot as you'll find, and you can take a variety of **hikes** inland to see a side of Antigua overlooked by the vast majority of tourists. Just southwest of St John's, the **Five Islands** peninsula holds several hotels, some good beaches and the substantial ruins of the eighteenth-century **Fort Barrington**.

> For details of accommodation on Antigua's west coast, see p.97; for eating and drinking see p.113.

LIBERTA AND SWETES

Map 2, E5.

Heading west from Falmouth, the first main village that you run into is **LIBERTA**, the first "free village" established for emancipated slaves after the abolition of slavery in 1834. It's still one of the largest settlements on the island, though you'll find little reason to stop off and explore. Beyond Liberta, **SWETES** is best known as the birthplace of cricketer Curtley Ambrose, the West Indies' leading fast bowler during the 1990s. If you happen to be there while Curtley is in action, listen out for a tolling bell – his mother's invariable way of informing the village that her son has taken a wicket.

**For more on the Antiguan
passion for cricket, see p.140.**

FIG TREE HILL

Map 2, F6.

Heading west at Swetes, you can follow the main road through the most densely forested part of the island, **Fig Tree Hill**. You won't actually see any fig trees – the road is lined with bananas (known locally as figs) and mango trees as it carves its way through some gorgeous scenery down to the south coast at Old Road. About halfway along the drive, you can stop at a small roadside shack which grandly calls itself the **Antigua Cultural Centre**, where you can get a drink and some fruit picked straight off the trees.

A track leads inland from the centre to the **Potworks Dam Reservoir** – the island's first – where you'll find picnic tables set up around the edge of the water. More serious hikers can take the **Rendezvous Trail**, which crosses the **Wallings Woodlands**, through mahogany trees and lush forest to the always empty beach a two-hour walk away at Rendezvous Bay (see p.60). Ask at the centre for a map or directions – the main path is little used and can quickly become overgrown and hard to make out.

There's an easier hike to the fabulous Rendezvous Bay from Falmouth on the south coast – see p.60.

OLD ROAD

Map 2, F6.

Once an important port and town, **OLD ROAD** derived its name from nearby Carlisle Bay – a safe anchorage or "road" for the early settlers – but was soon surpassed by the new "roads" of St John's and Falmouth Harbour. Today Old Road is a small and rather impoverished fishing village, enlivened by the swanky *Curtain Bluff* resort that hangs dramatically above the sea – and a superb swathe of beach – on the eponymous sandstone bluff.

BOGGY PEAK

Map 2, G5.

Heading west from Old Road, the road follows the coast past a series of banana groves and pineapple plantations and around **Cades Bay**, offering delightful views out to sea over Cades Reef. On the right, a kilometre from Old Road, a track leads up into the Shekerley Mountains to **Boggy Peak**, at 400 metres, the highest point on the island. The panoramic view from the top – in good visibility you can even make out St Kitts, Guadeloupe and Montserrat – is well worth the steep drive or the one-hour climb. Unfortunately, the peak is now occupied by a communication station, safely tucked away behind a high security fence, so you'll need to make arrangements to visit with Cable & Wireless in St John's (✆462 0840). If you haven't the time or the inclination, the views from outside the perimeter fence are almost as good.

DARKWOOD BEACH

Map 2, H5.

Continuing west through the village of **Urlings**, the road runs alongside a number of excellent beaches, including **Darkwood**, a great spot to stop and take a swim. The snorkelling here is excellent – look out for small underwater canyons just offshore, and schools of squid and colourful reef fish. Beachcombers will find this one of the best places on the island to look for shells and driftwood. There are a couple of groves of casuarina trees for shade, and a friendly little beach bar that offers inexpensive local food.

Jolly Harbour

Covering an immense area (much of it reclaimed swampland and saltponds) north of Darkwood, the 450-bedroom all-inclusive *Club Antigua* hotel sprawls alongside a mile of one of Antigua's best beaches. Adjacent, the **Jolly Harbour** complex has a marina, rental apartments, a golf course, restaurants and a small shopping mall. It's a world apart from the "real" Antigua – like a small piece of America transplanted in the Caribbean.

GREEN CASTLE HILL

Map 2, F4.

If you haven't climbed Boggy Peak (see p.73) or Monk's Hill (see p.61), you could consider getting your panoramic view of Antigua from the top of **Green Castle Hill**. The peak is littered with stone pillars and large rocks, claimed periodically as Stone-Age megaliths left by Antigua's oldest inhabitants. The claim is patently absurd – there is no evidence of Antigua's Amerindians having either the technology or the inclination to erect such monuments to their deities – but don't let that put you off visiting. The views are superb, particularly to the north beyond St John's and, the odd goat aside, you won't see a soul around.

You'll really need a car to get there. Head inland from the main road between Jennings and St John's towards Emanuel; the path to the top (a 40-minute walk) begins by the gates of a small brick factory connected to a large stone quarry.

FIVE ISLANDS

Map 2,G3.

To the west of St John's the highway leads out through a narrow isthmus onto the large **Five Islands** peninsula, named after five small rocks that jut from the sea just off-shore. There are several hotels, especially on the peninsula's northern coast, though the interior is largely barren and scrubby, and there's not a huge amount to see. A kilometre offshore from **Hawksbill Bay**, a large rock in the shape of the head of a hawksbill turtle gives the place its name.

On **Goat Hill,** at the northern point of the peninsula close to the *Royal Antiguan* hotel, the circular stone ruins of **Fort Barrington** overlook the gorgeous **Deep Bay**. The British first built a simple fort here in the 1650s, to protect the southern entrance to St John's Harbour; it was captured by the French when they took the city in 1666. In 1779, at a time of renewed tension between the two nations, Admiral Barrington of the British navy enlarged and strengthened the fort. This time, the deterrent proved effective; like most of Antigua's defences, Fort Barrington never saw any further action, and spent the next two centuries as a signal station reporting on the movement of ships in the local waters. It's well worth the 20-minute walk around the beach to the fort for the dramatic sense of isolation as you look out to sea or back over the tourists sunning themselves far below on the bay.

Barbuda and Redonda

With its magnificent and often deserted beaches, its spectacular coral reefs and its rare colony of frigate-birds, the nation's other inhabited island, **Barbuda** – 48km to the north of Antigua – is well worth a visit. Don't expect the same facilities as on Antigua; **accommodation** options are limited, you'll need to bring your own snorkelling or diving gear, and you'll find that schedules – whether for taxis, boats or meals – tend to drift. This is all, of course, very much part of the island's attraction.

Barbuda is a throbbing metropolis, however, compared with Antigua's other "dependency", the tiny and now uninhabited volcanic rock known as **Redonda**, some 56km to the southwest in the main chain of the Lesser Antilles, between Nevis and Guadeloupe.

Barbuda

Half the size of its better-known neighbour, **Barbuda** developed quite separately from Antigua and was only reluctantly coerced into joining the nation during the run-up to independence in 1981. The island is very much the "poor neighbour" in terms of financial resources, and its development has been slow; tourism has made only a minor impact, and fishing and farming remain the principal occupations of the tiny population of 1500, most of whom live in the small capital, **Codrington**.

The island is edged with powdery white-sand **beaches**, fringing an impossibly turquoise sea laced with coral reefs, perfect for snorkelling, diving and fishing. Along almost the entire length of the island's west coast run the mangrove swamps of **Codrington Lagoon**, home to the fabulous frigate birds. The **interior** is less fetching, mostly low-level scrub of cacti, bush, small trees and the distinctive century plants; for most of the year it is extremely arid and unwelcoming. There are a couple of exceptions: in the **southwest** the island suddenly bursts to life, with a fabulous grove of coconut palms springing out of the sandy soil (and providing a useful source of export revenue), while in parts of the **interior** government projects are reclaiming land from the bush to grow peanuts and sweet potatoes, also for the export market. For the most part, though, the island is left to the scrub, the elusive wild boar and deer and a multitude of birds – 170 species at last count.

Some history

Barbuda was first settled by a handful of English colonists in the 1620s, but the poor soil of this "barren rock", combined with attacks from Carib Indians from nearby islands, soon drove them off. Instead, livestock was released onto the island and periodically collected to feed the settlers on Antigua, St Kitts and Montserrat. In 1685 the English leased the island to the Codrington family, who were to hold it as private property for nearly 200 years. They continued to raise livestock for supplying both their sugar estates in Antigua and the Royal Navy at English Harbour (see p.62).

BARBUDA

Shipwrecks

The shallows around Barbuda are littered with **shipwrecks**, the last resting place of some 150 vessels that failed to navigate safely through its dangerous coral reefs. **Salvage** from the wrecks was an important income for the islanders from at least 1695, when the *Santiago de Cullerin* ran aground with 13,000 pesos, destined for paying the garrisons on the Spanish Main in South America. During the following century ships hitting the reefs included slavers, cargo ships and warships, with the Barbudans recovering everything from cases of brandy to dried codfish, sugar and coal. Income from salvage reached a peak of around £7000 a year by the early 1800s, though improved navigation techniques during the following century saw the number of wrecks decline sharply.

None of the Codringtons ever lived on Barbuda, leaving management to a local "governor", who supervised a slave population that reached 500 at its peak. However, defences were erected, including a castle and a martello tower, and a large house was built on the "Highlands", the ruins still evident today. Unlike Antigua, where slaves led a miserable existence chained to the sugar plantations, those in Barbuda had a relatively independent lifestyle, working as herdsmen, hunters, fishermen and shepherds. In the 1820s, an admittedly partisan Codrington wrote that his Barbuda slaves were "more happy, better fed and clothed and better off than the generality of peasants in England".

After emancipation of the slaves in 1834, the island remained privately owned until 1903, when it was adopted by the British Crown and administered alongside Antigua. In the run-up to independence in 1981, Barbudans made it clear that they wanted to remain independent of Antigua.

Unfortunately for them, Britain sided with Antigua, and Barbuda took on its present status as a semi-autonomous dependency of its sister island, with its own elected council and a representative in the Antiguan parliament.

Getting there and getting around

The only scheduled **flights** to Barbuda are from Antigua on LIAT, who offer two flights a day (presently leaving at 8.35am and 4pm) and charge US$50 round-trip. The Twin Otter 19-seater planes take 15 minutes and turn straight around for the return journey. More excitingly, the journey can be made by **boat**, although the cost of the 4–5hr crossing from St John's to River Landing on Barbuda's south coast tends to be pretty exorbitant; ask around with the charter companies (see p.19).

If you visit independently, getting around is likely to be your major headache. There is no bus service, and distances (and the heat) are sufficient to put all but the hardiest off the idea of walking anywhere. Also, you've no guarantee of finding one of the island's tiny **taxi** fleet in action, so it's worth calling ahead to try to **rent a jeep**: Mr Williams (©460 0047) can usually oblige for around US$50 per day. Alternatively, ask around at the airport for someone to give you a ride – there's usually a crowd there to meet the LIAT flights.

Taking a **day tour** to the island is the best way to guarantee getting both a driver and a boat operator to take you to the bird sanctuary. Earl's Tours (©462 0742 or 462 5647) will organize a carefully packaged day tour for $130, including flights, pick-up at Barbuda airport, a jeep tour of the island, lunch and a boat visit to the bird sanctuary. Your driver will also leave you on the beach for as long as you want – just remember to take a bottle of water. LIAT (©462 0700) offer similar tours.

BARBUDA

For details of accommodation in
Barbuda, see p.99;
for eating and drinking, see p.115.

CODRINGTON

Map 6, C5.

CODRINGTON, the island's capital and only settlement, holds almost the entire population of 1500 people within its grid of narrow streets. It's a well spread out place, with plenty of brightly painted single-storey clapboard or concrete buildings. There are a couple of guesthouses, a handful of restaurants, bars and supermarkets, but, for the most part, people keep to themselves, and there is little sign of life apart from a few curious schoolchildren, dogs and the occasional goat.

Codrington Lagoon

To the west of town, **Codrington Lagoon** is an expansive area of green, brackish water, fringed by mangroves. The lagoon is completely enclosed on its western side by the narrow but magnificent strip of **Palm Beach**, 22 kilometres long, but there is a narrow cut to the north where fishing boats can get out to the ocean. Lobsters breed in the lagoon and you'll probably see them at the pier being loaded for export to Antigua – an important contribution to the local economy. Equally significant – for this is what is starting to bring in the tourists – a series of mangrove clumps to the northwest of the lagoon, known as **Man of War Island**, provides the home and breeding ground for the largest group of frigate birds anywhere in the Caribbean (see box).

CODRINGTON

Frigate birds

You'll need a boat to get anywhere near the **frigate birds**, motoring out to the edge of the shallows where they live and then poling the boat punt-like to their nests. The sight as you approach is quite spectacular – the mothers will take to the skies as you draw near, joining the multitude of birds wheeling above you, and leaving their babies standing imperiously on the nest but watching you closely out of the corner of their eyes. The display gets even more dramatic during the mating season, from late August to December, when hundreds of the males put on a grand show – puffing up their bright red throat pouches as they soar through the air just a few metres above the females, watching admiringly from the bushes.

Small boats leave for the sanctuary from the main pier just outside Codrington and charge around US$45–50 per boat. If you just turn up without notice, there is no guarantee that you'll find someone to take you out, so it's advisable to visit as part of a tour or to make arrangements through your hotel or car rental.

AROUND THE ISLAND

To be frank, apart from any beach or snorkelling stops, a tour of the island is a pretty brief affair. Away from the lagoon, there are few "sights" as such – they are certainly not the reason you are here – and they're all pretty missable unless you're determined to get your money's worth.

North of Codrington a series of dirt roads fans out across the upper part of the island. One of these leads into the heart of the island, to the scant remains of **Highlands**

House, the castle the first Codringtons built on the island in the seventeenth century. The home must have been pretty extensive, for the ruins – crumbling walls and the occasional piece of staircase – cover a wide area. The views across the island from here are as panoramic as you'll find.

The caves

Map 6, D3.

Another dirt road leads up to the northeastern side of the island, where a series of **caves** has been naturally carved into the low cliffs. These are thought to have sheltered Taino and possibly Carib Indians in the centuries preceding the arrival of Europeans in the island. Scarce evidence of their presence has been found here, however, except for some unusual **petroglyphs**. The entrance to the main cave is opposite a large boulder, with the ruins of an old **watchtower** built up alongside. You'll need to scramble up the rocks for five minutes, then make a short, stooped walk inside the cave to reach the petroglyphs – a couple of barely distinguishable and very amateurish faces carved into the rockface. What is more noticeable is where pieces of rock have been prised away, a decade or so ago, by tourist vandals eager for their own chunk of ancient art. Alongside the petroglyphs, a large dome-shaped chamber – the "presidential suite" – was probably the main home of the Indians within the complex.

River Fort

Map 6, C6.

You can clamber around some more substantial remains at the **River Fort** in the southwest of the island, just beyond the coconut grove. The fort provides a surprisingly large defence for an island of Barbuda's size and importance. The island was attacked by Carib Indians in the 1680s and by the French navy in 1710, but there was too little valuable property here to tempt any further assailants into braving the dangerous surrounding reefs. As a result, the fort never saw any action, and its main role has been as a lookout and a landmark for ships approaching the island from the south.

The remains are dominated by a **Martello tower**, one of the many built throughout the British empire during the Napoleonic Wars on the plan of a tower at Cape Mortella in Corsica – hence their name. Right below the tower, the **River Landing** is the main point for access to Barbuda by boat and is always busy with trucks stockpiling and loading sand onto barges to be taken to replenish beaches in Antigua – a controversial but lucrative industry for the Barbudans.

For details on boat trips from Antigua, see p.79.

Spanish Point

Map 6, G8.

East of here the road leads out past the luxurious *K Club* hotel to the isolated **Spanish Point**, where a small finger of land divides the choppy waters of the Atlantic from the calm Caribbean Sea. Maps indicate a castle on Spanish Point, but if you make the effort to get there all you'll find are the ruins of a small lookout post. More interestingly, there is a marine reserve just offshore at **Palaster Reef**, where numerous shipwrecks have been located in the shallows amid the fabulous coral and abundant reef fish. You can swim to the edges of the reef from the beach, so don't forget your snorkelling or diving gear.

AROUND THE ISLAND

Barbuda's beaches

Invariably deserted, Barbuda's **beaches** are simply stunning. On the west coast, on the far side of Codrington Lagoon (and so only really accessible by boat), the gently curving **Palm Beach** offers 22km of dazzling white sand interspersed with long stretches of pink, created by the tiny fragments of millions of seashells washed up over the years. There's little shade here, so ask your boatman to drop you near one of the groves of casuarinas tree; he'll come back for you a few hours later.

On the east coast, the attractively named **Rubbish Bay** and **Hog Bay** are littered with driftwood and other detritus washed up by the Atlantic Ocean and offer great opportunities for beachcombing, while at many other places around the island you'll spot tiny bays and coves where you can jump out of your car for a private swim and some snorkelling.

Redonda

The little island of **Redonda** – a two-kilometre hump of volcanic rock rising a sheer 300 metres from the sea – was spotted and named by Columbus in 1493, but subsequently ignored for nearly four centuries. During the 1860s, however, valuable phosphate was found in bird guano there, and Redonda was promptly annexed by Antigua. Mining operations were begun, producing around 4000 tons a year by the end of the century. Output declined after World War I, the mining ceased, and the island has been unoccupied – except by goats and seabirds – since 1930.

Almost surreally, though, Redonda is still claimed as an **independent kingdom**. In 1865 a Montserratian sea-trader

Blue striped grunts and snappers amid the offshore coral reefs

Sunset behind English Harbour

The southwest coastal road

A secluded cove on Antigua catches the last of the evening sun

Driftwood on Ffryes Beach, Antigua

A banana plantation near Falmouth

Snorkelling off Barbuda

A calm, deserted beach on Barbuda

Matthew Shiell led an expedition to the island and staked his claim to it. His objections to Antigua's annexation of the island were ignored, but it didn't stop him from abdicating in favour of his novelist son in 1880; he in turn passed the fantasy throne to the English poet John Gawsworth, who took the title Juan III and appointed a number of his friends as nobles of the realm, including Dorothy L. Sayers, J.B. Priestley and Lawrence Durrell. Today, Leo V claims to have inherited the kingdom, using his title to promote the literary works of his predecessors, though at least one pretender to the throne argues that Gawsworth had abdicated in his favour during a night of heavy drinking at his local pub back in England.

Redonda is occasionally visited by yachtsmen – though with no sheltered anchorage, the landing is a difficult one – but there is no regular service to the island, nor anywhere to stay save a few ruined mining buildings when you get there.

LISTINGS

Accommodation

Antigua offers plenty of good **accommodation**, but there are also a lot of places that are complacent and overpriced. Prices tend to be high – the country seems to have made a decision to stay relatively "upmarket" in its tourism – which means that you're usually better off arranging accommodation as part of a package in advance.

Accommodation price codes

All accommodation listed in this guide has been graded according to the following price categories:

① Under US$40 ② US$40–60 ③ US$60–80
④ US$80–110 ⑤ US$110–150 ⑥ US$150–200
⑦ US$200 and above

Rates are for the cheapest available double or twin room during the high season – normally mid-December to mid-April. During the low season, rates are liable to fall by as much as 25 percent (though this is rare at the cheapest places), and proprietors are far more amenable to bargaining. Many of the all-inclusive hotels have a minimum stay requirement, and rates are quoted per person per night based on double occupancy.

Bear in mind that the prices quoted below are the maximum – particularly outside the winter season, most places will reduce their prices if you plead necessity, and some will do the same all year round. Bear in mind also that every place will add government tax of 8.5 percent to the bill and the majority will also impose a service charge of 10 percent. All places listed are on the beach unless mentioned otherwise.

ST JOHN'S

St John's is a fair way from a decent beach, so the majority of people who stay here are either on business or after the island's cheapest budget accommodation. There are a couple of good-value guesthouses but, if you've got the money, you'll probably prefer to stay out of town near some sand.

Barrymore Hotel
Map 2, F3. ℘462 1055, fax 462 4062.
Unremarkable but pleasant enough place, carved up into low-level pink units 15 minutes' walk from town and from the beach. There's a moderate-sized pool, a small gym, decent rooms and an attractive restaurant and bar.④

Heritage Hotel
Map 3, D3. Heritage Quay, ℘462 1247, fax 462 1179.
Right by the cruise-ship pier, a decent option if you're in town on business, otherwise completely missable. Spacious if rather drab rooms, all with their own well-equipped kitchens.④

Joe Mike's Hotel
Map 3, E4. Nevis Street, ℘462 1142, fax 462 6056.
Just a dozen rooms in this friendly place, right in the centre of town. Again, nothing special but handy if you want to spend a night in the city.②

All-inclusives

The latest trend in hotel accommodation in the Caribbean has been towards **"all-inclusive" hotels**, and Antigua is no exception. The simple concept behind these places is that you pay a single price that covers your room, all meals and, normally, all drinks and watersports, so you can "leave your wallet at home". Heavily pushed by travel agents (who take a commission on the total price), all-inclusives really took off in the troubled Jamaica of the 1980s, where many tourists were nervous about leaving their hotel compound at all. Their relevance for an island like Antigua is questionable.

From the local point of view, the problem with all-inclusives is their effect on the independent sector. Local establishments lose custom because guests are tied to their hotel, reluctant to leave it and pay "twice" for food, drink or windsurfing. Nonetheless, all-inclusivity is the flavour of the month in Antigua, with several hotels recently jumping on the bandwagon, and hordes of repeat visitors at places like Sandals.

If you're thinking of booking an all-inclusive, focus on what you specifically want out of it. Sandals and the giant Club Antigua, for example, have several restaurants and bars, so you don't have to face the same menu every night; smaller places like Rex Blue Heron offer less variety, but a bit more space on the beach. Remember, too, that the allure of drinking seven types of "free" cocktail in a night or stuffing your face at the "free" buffet quickly fades, especially if you want to get out and sample Antigua's great restaurants and bars.

Spanish Main

Map 3, G3. Independence Drive, ✆462 0660.
Attractive eighteenth-century inn, claimed as the one-time home of the island's British governor, with fourteen simple and

slightly cramped rooms, each with a small private bathroom. Nothing spectacular, and it can be a bit noisy, but superb value year-round.①

THE NORTHWEST COAST

Antigua's **northwest coast** is the most popular destination for visitors, with a series of large and small hotels dotted along the lovely beaches of **Runaway Bay** and **Dickenson Bay**. This is the place to come for action, with plenty of restaurants, watersports and beach life, though you usually only need a short walk to find a bit of privacy, even during high season. Badly hit by Hurricane Luis in 1995 (see p.53), Runaway Bay is the quieter of the two, with fewer vendors and a less well maintained beach.

RUNAWAY BAY

Barrymore Beach Club
Map 4, C6. PO Box 1774, ② and fax 462 4101.
A reasonable option on a small piece of land with its own tiny, virtually private beach, a quiet, secluded feel and comfortable if unspectacular rooms, studios and one-bedroom apartments. ⑤

Dove Cove
Map 4, Z9. ②463 8600, fax 462 5907.
Modern, spacious one- and two-bedroom apartments with full kitchens and cable TV. The drawback is that the place is a bit cut-off, five minutes' walk from the beach and ten minutes' drive from St John's, but the owners offer good-value deals that include the accommodation and car hire.⑤

Sandhaven Beach Resort
Map 4, A9. ② and fax, 462 4491.
Excellent, low-cost and refreshingly unpretentious option at

the southern end of Runaway Bay, with a wide stretch of clean, white beach and decent snorkelling just offshore. The rooms are rustic and simple, though perfectly adequate, all fourteen of them face out to sea, and there's a good, reasonably priced beachside restaurant on-site. On the downside, the place is a long walk (or a US$6 taxi ride) from any other tourist facilities and the ocean view is marred a bit by the oil-pumping station 3km offshore, but this is as good value as you'll find on the island.④

Sunset Cove Resort
Map 4, C6. PO Box 1262, ✆462 3762, fax 462 2684.
Situated at the northern end of the bay, the hotel lost its beach entirely in heavy sea swells in late 1996, and you have to walk five minutes around the headland to swim comfortably. That problem aside, it's a very pleasant place, attractively landscaped and with a small freshwater pool, and the rooms are sizeable and all have kitchen facilities and cable TV. There is also a restaurant and small nightclub on-site.⑤

Time Away Apartments
Map 4, C5. PO Box 189, ✆462 1212, fax 462 2587.
Right next to *Sunset Cove* and suffering from the same beach erosion, this little block offers six decent one-bedroom apartments with tiled floors, rattan furniture and self-catering facilities.④

DICKENSON BAY

Antigua Village Condo Beach Resort
Map 4, E4. PO Box 649, ✆462 2930, fax 462 0375.
Large if unremarkable resort with dozens of self-catering apartments – from studios to two-bedroom flats – strewn around attractively landscaped gardens. There's a small swimming pool and a grocery store on site.⑤

DICKENSON BAY

Marina Bay Beach Resort

Map 4, C5. PO Box 1187, ✆462 3254, fax 462 2151.
Unmistakeable salmon-pink buildings overlooking a small marina on the southern edge of Dickenson Bay. Rooms are bright, tastefully furnished and as spacious as you'll find, with good self-catering facilities and cable TV in each. The views over the marina and out to sea are OK, though not as grand as you'll find elsewhere.④

Rex Halcyon Cove

Map 4, F3. PO Box 251, ✆462 0256, fax 462 0271.
Very large, sprawling low-rise resort at the northern end of the beach, rather faded and a little time-worn but with good-sized rooms, a decent pool and tennis courts and a delightful restaurant on the Warri pier (see p.109).⑤

Sandals Antigua

Map 4, F4. PO Box 147, ✆462 0267, fax 462 4135.
Superbly designed, always lively, couples-only all-inclusive, part of a Jamaican-owned chain that has taken the Caribbean by storm in the last decade. The 189 luxury rooms are cleverly spread throughout the resort, reducing the sense of being part of a crowd, and four restaurants offer excellent Italian, Japanese, southern US and international food, as well as a couple of 24-hour snack bars. All watersports, including diving (training, certification and dives) are included in the price. There's a minimum stay of three nights.⑦

Siboney Beach Club

Map 4, E4. PO Box 222, ✆462 0806, fax 462 3356.
Small, intimate and very friendly place, fabulously landscaped in a micro-jungle of its own. Rooms are spacious and comfortable.⑥

THE NORTHEAST

Antigua's **northeast** is pretty quiet from the tourist point of view, with fewer hotels, restaurants, shopping facilities and good beaches than you'll find further west. That said, there are a couple of hotels that are as good value as you'll find anywhere, though you'll probably want a car – at least for a couple of days – to make up for being so far from the action.

Antigua Sugar Mill Hotel
Map 2, E2. Airport Rd, PO Box 319 ©462 3044, fax 462 1500.
Faded hotel, five minutes from the airport and ten from the nearest beach, short on atmosphere but with comfortable enough rooms and a small swimming-pool.④

Colonna Beach Resort
Map 2, F1. Hodges Bay, PO Box 951 ©462 6263, fax 462 6430.
The most attractive of the large north coast resorts, Mediterranean in design – red-tiled roofs and pastel shades throughout – well-landscaped, and with the biggest and most spectacular pool on the island. The beach is pretty ordinary, and you're some way from the island's main action, but the solitude is addictive (though the hotel itself can get quite crowded).⑥

Lord Nelson Beach Hotel
Map 2, E2. Dutchman's Bay, ©462 3094, fax 462 0751.
Small, friendly place, popular with windsurfers – who catch on to the onshore winds that keep the place pleasantly cool for much of the year – but also great value for those who want a quiet place on a decent beach to escape the crowds.④

Vienna Inn
Map 2, F1. Hodges Bay, © and fax 462 1442.
Austrian-owned, big, yellow wooden house, divided up into reasonable but fairly basic rooms and apartments by the sea, a couple of minutes' walk from the nearest beach.③

EAST COAST

Staying on the **east coast**, you'll feel a long way from any-where – a car is essential for getting out and seeing the island – but the hotels are extremely pleasant and it's very quiet.

Long Bay Hotel
Map 2, C3. Long Bay, ✆463 2005, fax 463 2439.
Small all-inclusive in a fabulous setting by a tiny turquoise bay, with 20 cosy cottages and a real feeling of isolation.⑦

Pineapple Beach Club
Map 2, C3. Long Bay, ✆463 2006, fax 463 2452.
Sprawling but beautifully landscaped all-inclusive, with 130 rooms scattered beside a lovely stretch of beach.⑦

ENGLISH HARBOUR AND FALMOUTH

Plenty of good restaurants and nightlife and the proximity of the **Nelson's Dockyard** make this an attractive area to stay, though if you're after serious beaches you'll want to look elsewhere on the island.

Admiral's Inn
Map 5, E5. Nelson's Dockyard, ✆460 1153, fax 460 1534.
Built in 1788 as the dockyard's supply store and now attractive-ly restored, this is one of the best accommodation options in Antigua, with great atmosphere, welcoming staff, a romantic setting by the harbour and sensible prices.⑤

Catamaran Hotel
Map 5, C1. Falmouth, ✆460 1036, fax 460 1506.
Friendly little place on the north side of the harbour in Falmouth, adjacent to a small marina. The beach is not great

for swimming and it's a bit of a hike to the action at the dock-yard, but the rooms are comfortable and good value.④

Copper and Lumber Store

Map 5, E5. Nelson's Dockyard, ©460 1058, fax 460 1529.

Very elegant Georgian hotel in the heart of the dockyard, used from the late eighteenth century as its name suggests, with a dozen superb rooms – some fabulously furnished with mostly nautically themed antiques. ⑥

Falmouth Harbour Beach Apartments

Map 5, D4. Falmouth ©460 1027, fax 460 1534.

Reasonably sized self-catering studio apartments with ceiling fans and ocean-front verandas on the east side of the harbour by a thin strip of beach. Nothing spectacular but decent value.⑤

The Inn on English Harbour

Map 5, F5. English Harbour, ©460 1041, fax 460 1450.

Attractive old hotel, spread over a large site beside the harbour next to a pleasant white sand beach.⑦

Harbour View Apartments

Map 5, C1. Falmouth, ©460 1762, fax 460 1871.

Modern block with six two-bed self-catering apartments by a small and unexceptional beach.⑤

WEST COAST

Antigua's **west coast** has more hotel rooms than any other part of the island, and a combination of low-, mid-, and off-the-scale high-end options to choose from. The *Club Antigua* hotel and adjoining *Jolly Harbour Beach Resort* form a huge community in the centre of the coast, complete with restaurants, bars and shopping mall.

Club Antigua

Map 2, G5. Lignum Vitae Bay, ✆462 0061, fax 462 4900.

Vast all-inclusive resort – 480 rooms scattered along half a kilo-metre of good, white beach – with four restaurants, six bars, a disco, a small casino, tennis courts and free watersports (training and rental), including windsurfing, waterskiing, small sailboats and paddle boats. In a place this size, you can't avoid feeling part of a big crowd, and the food is nothing to write home about, but on the whole the place offers pretty decent value. All-inclusive rates per couple start at US$216/190 in winter/summer.⑦

Jolly Harbour Beach Resort

Map 2, G5. Jolly Harbour, ✆462 6166, fax 462 6167.

Modern complex of about fifty waterfront villas, mostly two-bedroomed with a full kitchen and a balcony overlooking the harbour. Plenty of shops, restaurants and sports facilities nearby, but the place is still being developed and feels somewhat bland.④

Curtain Bluff

Map 2, F6. Old Road, ✆462 8400, fax 462 8409.

For the seriously rich only, a spectacular all-inclusive hotel built on the craggy bluff that overlooks Carlisle Bay and Cades Reef. Rates include all meals and drinks, scuba diving, sailing on the hotel's private yacht and a host of other top-class facilities.⑦

Hawksbill Beach

Map 2, G3. Five Islands, ✆462 0301, fax 462 1515.

Attractive hotel that sprawls over a vast area on the Five Islands peninsula, overlooking the bay and the jagged rock – shaped like the beak of a hawksbill turtle – that pokes from the sea and gives the place its name. Four beaches, dramatic views, lovely landscaped gardens and a restored sugar mill converted into a store all add to the atmosphere.⑦

WEST COAST

Rex Blue Heron

Map 2, G6. Johnson's Point, ✆462 8564, fax 462 8564.
Medium-sized all-inclusive on one of the best west-coast beaches, with comfortable rooms and a small pool a stone's throw from the sea.⑤

Royal Antiguan

Map 2, G3. Deep Bay, ✆462 3733, fax 462 3732.
At nine storeys this massive and rather ugly place feels like a big-city business hotel accidentally plonked down in the middle of the Caribbean. That said, the facilities are excellent, particularly for tennis and watersports, the rooms are comfortable and the beach busy but pleasant, and if you can get a decent rate as part of a package it's not a bad place to stay if you can handle the crowd.⑤

Yepton Beach Resort

Map 2, G3. Deep Bay, ✆462 2520, fax 462 3240.
Nothing flash, but a pleasantly landscaped and welcoming little resort, with its own supply of windsurfers and small sailboats, and the occasional bout of entertainment – live bands, etc – thrown in for the guests. The rooms are good sizes and most have a full kitchen.⑥

BARBUDA

Accommodation on the quiet and undeveloped island of **Barbuda** ranges from the rustic to the luxurious, but all of them, whatever the price bracket, offer decent value. Always call ahead to book, and remember to bring mosquito repellent.

Earl's Villas

Map 6, C5. Codrington, ✆462 5647, fax 462 0742.
Pleasant, self-catering one-storey guesthouse just south of town.

BARBUDA

Accommodating up to eight people, it's ideal for families, but can also be divided up and used as separate flats sharing the same kitchen.③

K Club
Map 6, E7. Cocoa Point, ℂ460 0300, fax 460 0305.
Closed June–Nov.
Stunning Italian-owned and designed place in the south of the island, a celebrity home from home with its own golf course and watersports facilities.⑦

Nedd's Guesthouse
Map 6, C5. Codrington, ℂ460 0059.
Just a handful of comfortable and airy rooms, with a kitchen and grocery store downstairs – if it's full, the owner should be able to direct you to someone who'll rent you a room.③

Eating and drinking

There are plenty of good **eating** options on Antigua and, though prices are generally on the high side, there's usually something to suit most budgets. Around most of the island, hotel and restaurant menus aimed at tourists tend to offer familiar variations on Euro-American style food, shunning local specialities – a real shame, as the latter are invariably excellent and well worth trying if you get the chance.

Many **restaurants** close for between one and three months over the summer, sometimes on a whim, depending on how quiet the season is expected to be. We've given phone numbers for these, and for those where booking is recommended, below. Government tax of 8.5 percent is always added and, particularly at the pricier places, a 10 percent service charge is also automatic.

For **drinking**, Wadadli is the local **beer**, a reasonable brew though not quite a match for the superb Red Stripe – Jamaican beer brewed under licence on the island. Other regular beers on offer include Heineken, Guinness and the Trinidadian Carib. **Rum** is the most

CHAPTER 7 • EATING AND DRINKING

101

Antiguan food

Almost everywhere, **breakfast** is based around coffee, cereal, toast and eggs, and will usually include fresh **fruit**, one of the country's strong points. Expect to find paw-paws, bananas and the sweet Antiguan black pineapple; in season – generally between May and August – you should also make a special effort to look out for the delicious local mangoes and sapodillas.

For other meals you'll find that **seafood** – as you'd expect – is one of the island's strongpoints. Of the fish, the tasty and versatile red snapper and grouper are the staples but, if you're lucky, you'll also find swordfish, mahi-mahi and the very meaty marlin on the menu. Lobster is usually the priciest item, anywhere from EC$45–85 depending on season and the type of establishment. You'll also find conch ("konk") – a large shellfish often curried or battered in fritters, though best of all eaten raw in conch salad, when it's finely chopped with hot and sweet peppers, cucumber and lemon juice – as well as the giant local cockles and whelks, usually served in a buttery garlic sauce.

Other Antiguan specialities include the fabulous **ducana** (grated sweet potato mixed with coconut and spices and steamed in a banana leaf), **pepperpot stew** with salt beef, pumpkin and okra, often served with a cornmeal pudding known as **fungi**, various types of **curry**, **salted codfish**, and **souse** – cuts of pork marinated in lime juice, onions, hot and sweet peppers and spices.

Vegetarians will find their choices strictly limited – there are some great vegetables grown in Antigua, including pumpkins, okra and the squash-like christophene, but many menus don't include a single vegetarian dish, and even the widely available rice and peas often contains a piece of salted pork.

Restaurant prices and reservations

In the reviews that follow, restaurants have been graded as inexpensive (under US$20 a head for a three-course meal without drinks), moderate (US$20–30), expensive (US$30–40) and very expensive (over US$40). During the winter season (Dec–April) it's worth making a reservation at many of the places recommended and, if you've got your heart set on a special place, arrange it a couple of days in advance if you can.

popular spirit, used as the basis for a range of cocktails from pina coladas to cuba libre (rum and coke). The English Harbour and Cavalier brands are both made on the island, though real aficionados of the stuff will want to look out for Mount Gay Extra Old from Barbados or the Haitian Barbancourt, both brilliant Caribbean rums, best served neat on ice.

Of the **soft drinks**, you'll find the usual brands of sodas across the island as well as the tasty sparkling grapefruit drink Ting, made locally. Look out for vendors standing by piles of green coconuts; for a couple of EC dollars they'll cut the top off one for you to drink the sweet, delicious milk.

ST JOHN'S

Although the chances are that you won't be staying in **St John's**, there's plenty of reason to head into town when it comes to chow-time. In *Julian's* and *Home*, the city has two of Antigua's best restaurants, and there are more than a dozen other good places offering a wider variety of choices than you'll find elsewhere on the island. As you'd expect in the capital, local cuisine is often excellent and well worth checking out; alternatively, international options include

ST JOHN'S

Mexican and Indian, with Redcliffe Quay in particular a good place to head for.

Café Decima

Map 3, D3. Lower High St.
Lunch only; closed Sun. Moderate
Tucked away off the road, a quiet moderately priced garden restaurant that makes a pleasant retreat from shopping or exploring during the day. There's usually at least one lunchtime local special, such as ducana or fungi with saltfish for around EC$25, while more standard chicken and fish meals cost around EC$40.

Chutneys

Map 2, F3. Fort Rd, ✆462 2977.
Tues–Sun dinner only; closed Mon. Moderate.
The only authentic Indian restaurant on the island, five minutes' drive north of town between *KFC* and *Pizza Hut*, serving a wide variety of chicken, lamb and seafood curries – from mild to highly spicy – as well as tandoori, tikka, rotis, and some excellent vegetable dishes.

Curry House

Map 3, D4. Redcliffe Quay.
Mon–Sat 10am–6pm; closed Sun. Inexpensive.
One of the small, renovated huts on the quay and a great spot for rotis during the day, with chicken or beef options for EC$12, conch or shrimp for EC$14 and vegetable rotis for EC$10. They also offer the same fillings, served with rice rather than in a roti, for an extra EC$2 per plate.

Hemingway's

Map 3, D3. St Mary's St, ✆462 2763.
Mon–Sat 8.30am–11pm; closed Sun. Moderate.
Atmospheric, early nineteenth-century green and white wooden building with a balcony overlooking the street and Heritage

Quay. Can be overwhelmingly popular when the cruise ships are in; at other times, it's a great place to be, serving a range of excellent food from sandwiches and burgers to fish and steak dinners.

Home Restaurant

Map 3, G1. Lower Gambles, ©461 7651.
Mon–Sat dinner only; closed Sun. Expensive.
Attractive restaurant in a converted home, a little way from the centre of town, serving great, adventurous West Indian food. Look for starters of roast peppers and beets in balsamic vinegar and garlic (EC$18), main courses of "Arawak duck" with pineapple, papaya and rum sauce (EC$59) or blackened redfish (EC$55).

The Hub

Map 3, E3. Soul Alley/Long St.
Mon–Sat 8am–7pm. Inexpensive.
Local eatery and sports bar, particularly good for lunch Antiguan-style, with daily specials including curried goat, pepperpot stew and mackerel with dumplings or bread-like johnny cakes, each for around EC$16.

Joe Mike's

Map 3, E4. Nevis St/Corn Alley.
Daily 7.30am–10pm. Inexpensive.
Unpretentious local eatery – a popular lunchtime haunt for government ministers and other prominent Antiguans – serving large portions of ducana and saltfish, stewed pork, fungi and lingfish or barbecued ribs, all for around EC$15-25. Seafood buffet for a rather more hefty US$23 per person, Thurs and Sat from 6pm.

Julian's

Map 3, E2. Corner of Church St and Corn Alley, ©462 4766.
Tues–Sun dinner only; closed Mon. Expensive–very expensive.
Some of the finest eating on the island, with English chef Julian

Waterer producing superb crossover European/Caribbean cooking in an intimate and attractively renovated eighteenth-century home. Starters of charred, blackened brie or warm shrimp and scallop salad begin at US$10, mains of pan-fried snapper, coq au vin or vegetarian crepes cost from US$18 to US$25. It's a welcoming place, with efficient service, and there's an extensive list of well-kept wine.

Margarita's

Map 3, D4. Redcliffe Quay.
Daily 11am–9pm. Moderate.
Decent Mexican food at sensible prices by the waterfront – chicken or vegetarian burritos and enchiladas from EC$15 and superb chicken fajitas for EC$25. Good spot for drinking, too, with several Mexican beers and the best margaritas in town, with mango, lime and regular options for EC$10. Reduced prices and free chips and salsa during happy hour (Mon–Fri 5–7pm).

Pizzas in Paradise

Map 3, D4. Redcliffe Quay
Closed Sun. Moderate.
Pub-like atmosphere, popular with tourists for lunch and early dinner, serving reasonable quality food inside or outdoors under the trees at decent prices – pizzas, salads and baked potatoes as well as more typical Antiguan fish and chicken meals from EC$15-35.

The Redcliffe Tavern

Map 3, D3. Redcliffe Quay, ©461 4557.
Mon–Sat 8am–9pm. Moderate.
Housed in one of the renovated quayside warehouses, the atmospheric tavern serves good American/Caribbean food all day, with options such as flying fish in beer batter, jerk chicken, creole shrimp and pan-fried mahi-mahi fish all for around US$15.

Russell's

Map 2, G3. Fort James, ℂ462 5479.

Daily for lunch and dinner. Moderate.

Spectacular open-air setting on the top of the old British Fort James, looking across the once formidably defended entrance to St John's harbour. The food's not bad, either: at lunchtime you can get creole chicken with rice for EC$25, various styles of fish for EC$30, while at night a more varied menu offers conch fritters, giant Antiguan cockles and burgers, all for around EC$20 and pan-fried snapper with fries or rice for EC$40.

Shooters

Map 3, E3. High St.

Daily from 9pm.

Often the most crowded bar in town, a psychedelic purple place above a large discount store, popular with Antiguans, expats and tourists alike, with a fine selection of beers and spirits.

Spanish Main

Map 3, G3. Independence Ave.

Daily 8am–9pm. Inexpensive–moderate.

Good food all day, with full English breakfasts for EC$20, lunchtime meat or vegetable rotis for EC$12, spinach and ricotta pasties for EC$20 and evening specials of chicken curry, dahl and rice, kingfish and potatoes or chicken Kiev, all for around EC$35. Sunday lunch – five roast meats and all the trimmings for EC$45 – is excellent and very popular.

THE NORTH AND EAST

With a wide range of hotels dotted around the **north coast** there is a steady stream of punters looking for good places to eat, and plenty of decent restaurants have popped up as a result, though there are few options in the low budget range. **Dickenson Bay** has the widest choice, including the magnificent *Coconut Grove*, but, if you're staying around the coast in the northeast, you'll need to travel a bit if you want to vary your options. Further **east**, the hotels are all-inclusive so, with all the guests already catered for, there is virtually no room for an independent restaurant. Accordingly, don't plan to eat dinner out there unless you you want to buy an evening pass to one of the hotels.

RUNAWAY BAY AND DICKENSON BAY

Coconut Grove

Map 4, E4. *Siboney Beach Club*, Dickenson Bay, ✆462 1538.
Daily 11am–2pm & 6–9.30pm. Expensive–very expensive.
One of the top food choices on the island – superb cooking and friendly service at a delightful open-air beachside location. Mouth-watering starters set the tone – deep-fried jumbo shrimp in a coconut dip, succulent lobster cocktail, both around US$9 – followed by blackened swordfish in a banana salsa or creole snapper for US$23. Desserts include a magnificent coconut cream pie for US$8.50. If you're going to splash out just once in Antigua, this is a great choice.

The Lobster Pot

Map 4, C7. Runaway Bay, ✆462 2855.
Daily 7.30am–midnight. Moderate–expensive.
Good food served all day on a large beachfront covered veranda at the back of the old *Runaway Bay Hotel*, devastated by Hurricane Luis. Efficient and unobtrusive staff offer lunches of blackened fish, shrimp and chicken linguine or more basic chicken and burgers for US$10-15, while the evening meals include thick soups for US$4-5, catch of the day for US$15 and various lobster options starting at US$30.

Pari's Pizza

Map 4, G3. Dickenson Bay, ✆462 1501.
Closed Mon. Moderate.
Pizzas and ribs – nothing earth-shattering, and overpriced at EC$38 for a small rack of ribs, EC$29 for the smallest of the pizzas, but reasonable enough if you're staying nearby.

Spice of Life

Map 4, A9. *Sandhaven Hotel*, Runaway Bay, ✆462 4491.
Daily for lunch and dinner. Moderate.
With a three-course evening menu priced at US$23 – choose, for example, from starters of chicken livers or mussel soup and mains of pork in tarragon and mustard or chicken with pineapple – this is decent food at great value, served at the open-air beachside restaurant. There's an a la carte menu, too, and at lunchtime you can get burgers and sandwiches for around US$5, chicken or ribs with fries for US$13.

Spinnakers

Map 4, E4. Dickenson Bay, ✆462 4158.
Daily 7.30am–11pm. Expensive.
Reasonable option alongside the *Antigua Village Resort*, offering a decent, varied menu: dinner starters of crab backs (US$8.50, shrimp bisque (US$5) or deep fried camembert (US$6.50), and main courses of snapper en croute (US$25) or flying fish (US$13). Lunch involves burgers, pasta, ribs and crepes for US$8–12. The cooking is adequate if unspectacular, but the beachside location is undeniably attractive.

Warri Pier

Map 4, F3. *Rex Halcyon Cove*, Dickenson Bay, ✆462 0256.
Daily for lunch and dinner. Moderate–expensive.
Delightful open-air dining on a pier jutting out into the bay, with an option of sitting at small tables along the boardwalk or

RUNAWAY BAY AND DICKENSON BAY

at the main body of the pier. American staples dominate the lunch menu, with burgers and BLTs for US$6–8, with a more interesting evening selection of fresh fish and steaks at US$15–18.

NORTHEAST

Le Bistro,
Map 2, E1. Hodges Bay, ✆462 3881.
Tues–Sat dinner only; closed Mon. Expensive–very expensive.
Long-established restaurant serving good, reasonably authentic French food including starters of onion soup for EC$20 and snails in garlic butter for EC$25, main courses of lobster fettucine (EC$55), stir-fried shrimps flambéed in brandy (EC$70) and duck in orange sauce (EC$65).

Lord Nelson Beach Hotel
Map 2, E2. Dutchman's Bay.
Daily 7am–9pm. Inexpensive–moderate.
Large, welcoming place with a solid range of reasonably priced food all day, from soup, sandwiches and salads at lunchtime to local specialities and more typical European-style meals at night.

Sottovento
Map 2,E1. Next to *Colonna Beach Resort*, Hodges Bay, ✆462 6263.
Daily for lunch and dinner. Moderate–expensive.
Rock solid ocean-side Italian restaurant, with a decent value three-course "menu del giorno" for US$25 as well as a la carte options, including starters of conch salad or fettucine with pesto for US$10 and main dishes of veal scallopine, fresh fish or pasta for US$15–20.

The Beach Bar
Map 2, C3. Long Bay.
Daily, lunch only. Inexpensive.
Often lively local spot right on the beach, a great place to take a break from the sun and surf. Chicken and rice, burgers or fish and chips for EC$15-25.

ENGLISH HARBOUR AND AROUND

Abracadabra
Map 5, E5. Nelson's Dockyard, ✆460 2701.
Daily 11am–2pm & 6–11pm. Moderate–expensive.
Just outside the dockyard and offering a mostly Italian menu of pastas and grilled meat and fish, with a cosy atmosphere and live music several nights a week.

The Admiral's Inn
Map 5, E5. Nelson's Dockyard, ✆460 1027.
Daily 7am–9pm. Moderate.
Good, unpretentious dining in the old building or, more romantically, by the water's edge, with a selection of local dishes among the more standard fish and chicken meals.

The Dock
Map 5, E5. Nelson's Dockyard.
Daily 11am–2.30pm & 6–10pm. Moderate.
Overhanging the water, the Dock is a good place for a lunchtime snack of burgers, omelettes or sandwiches , or just to grab a drink at the enormous bar.

Dockyard Bakery
Map 5, E5. Nelson's Dockyard.
Daily 8am–5pm. Inexpensive.

The best place for breakfast or daytime snacks, selling guava danishes, pineapple turnovers and bread pudding, all freshly baked in the dockyard's old kitchens.

The Hideout
Map 2, 6D. Mamora Bay, ⓒ460 3666.
Fri–Wed, closed Thurs. Expensive–very expensive.
Expect to find interesting varieties of snapper, tuna and lobster at this friendly place, on the hill above Mamora Bay to the east of English Harbour, on the expensive side but a good option if you want to splash out.

Jackee's Kwik Stop
Map 5, E4. Falmouth Harbour.
Daily for lunch and dinner. Inexpensive.
One of the best of the local eateries run by the delightful Jackee, selling typical Antiguan food, with daily specials of ducana and saltfish, pepperpot and fungi or souse.

The Lookout
Map 5, G6. Shirley Heights.
Daily 10am–6pm. Moderate.
The only place for a refreshment break while you're up on the Heights, with a large patio providing superb views over the harbour and the dockyard. Simple meals are the order of the day, with the Sunday barbecue pulling a huge crowd for the reggae and steel bands that play from early afternoon through to the late evening.

The Mad Mongoose
Map 5, E4. Falmouth Harbour.
Daily 10am–11pm. Moderate.
Often lively bar, absolutely packed when the boats are in, serving snacks and simple meals a stone's throw from the water.

Al Porto

Map 2, G5. Jolly Harbour, ✆462 7695.
Daily 11am–2.30pm & 6–10.30pm. Moderate.
Popular Italian open-air eatery, in a lovely spot right by the
marina, with starters of mozzarella and tomatoes or chunky
soups for US$5-8, solid pizzas and pastas for US$10-15, and
grilled fish or steaks for US$20-25.

Chez Pascal

Map 2, G3. Galley Bay Hill, Five Islands, ✆462 3232.
Daily for lunch and dinner. Expensive.
Good French restaurant serving classy food in an intimate and
cosy setting. Pass the *Galley Bay Hotel*, take a right and then go
right again up a steep hill.

Co-Cos

Map 2, G5. Lignum Vitae Bay
Daily, dinner only. Expensive.
One of the most romantic spots on the island – a candlelit
terrace overlooking a gorgeous west-coast bay – and the
food's pretty good, too. Look for starters of pumpkin soup,
conch fritters or crab cakes for EC$12-16, and main courses
of baked tuna with red peppers or grouper fillet with lime for
EC$42-45.

Darkwood Beach Bar & Restaurant

Map 2, H5. Darkwood Beach
Daily, lunch only. Inexpensive.
A good place to grab some lunch if you're chilling out on this
excellent west coast beach, with a couple of hot dishes includ-
ing grilled chicken with peas and rice (EC$25) or steamed fish
(EC$40).

THE WEST COAST

Dogwatch Tavern

Map 2, G5. Jolly Harbour.

Daily 6–10pm. Inexpensive–moderate.

English-style pub with pool tables and dartboards, decorated with flags, pennants and sailing regalia, right beside the marina, with tables indoors and out, and a happy hour from 5.30-6.30pm. There's an inexpensive outdoor snack-bar and grill, with burgers for EC$20, hot dogs for EC$10, red snapper with peas and rice for EC$28, 8oz NY strip steak with fries for EC$45.

Peter's

Map 2, G5. Jolly Harbour.

Daily 5.30–10pm. Moderate–expensive.

Heavily meat-oriented barbeque zone overlooking the marina, with reasonable if unspectacular offerings of chicken breast or pork loin (EC$38), red snapper (EC$48) and steaks (EC$58-80), and an open salad bar (EC$22).

Turner's Rudder

Map 2, G6. Johnson's Point.

Daily 11am–2.30pm & 5.30–9pm. Inexpensive–moderate.

Delightful little restaurant on another of the best west coast beaches, a stone's throw from the *Blue Heron Hotel*. It's an unpretentious place, with plastic furniture right on the sand, but the cooking is good and the atmosphere mellow. The evening menu includes chicken kebabs (EC$25), red snapper fillet (EC$35) and grilled lobster (EC$55), as well as vegetable or chicken rotis (EC$10–15). During the day, you'll find the same menu, but even if you're not particularly hungry, it's a great place to retreat from the beach for a snack and a beer.

BARBUDA

K Club
Map 6, E7. ©460 0300.

Expensive–very expensive.

Spectacular place which, except at busy times, welcomes anyone visiting the island for lunch and dinner. Expect great food,
beautiful people, a fabulous setting and hefty prices.

Lagoon Café
Map 6, C5.

Inexpensive.

The main nightly hangout, a dimly lit place offering simple
meals, guys playing dominos and the (very) occasional live
band.

Palm Tree
Map 6 C5. ©460 0517.

Moderate.

Good Barbudan food, particularly for fish and lobster, but
you'll need to let them know that you're coming (preferably a
day in advance) and what you want to eat.

Music and nightlife

As you'd expect with Antigua's small population, the country doesn't offer a vast amount in the way of regular nightlife. There are only a couple of **night-clubs** on the island, one cinema and no regular theatres, though some of the best bars lay on occasional live **music**. We've listed the most likely places below, but you'll want to keep an eye open for flyers and radio and newspaper ads announcing where the live bands are going to be. If you're here in August, you'll find that the country's annual **Carnival** more than compensates for the quiet times.

ST JOHN'S AND THE NORTH

Deluxe Cinema
High St, St John's, ✆462 2188.
The island's only cinema, showing the latest imports from the USA.

King's Casino
Heritage Quay
Mon–Sat 10am–4am, Sun 6pm–4am.

Carnival

The highlight of Antigua's entertainment calendar is its **Carnival**, a colourful, exuberant party held for ten days, from late July until the first Tuesday in August. Warm-ups start in early July, with steel bands, calypsonians and deejays in action across the island, and carnival proper gets cracking with the opening of Carnival City at the Antigua Recreation Ground in St John's. This is where all of the scheduled events take place, though you'll often find spontaneous outbreaks of partying across the city, and a festival village is set up nearby to provide space for the masses of food and drink vendors who emerge out of nowhere.

Of the major carnival events, the **Panorama** steelband contest and the calypso monarch competition are both packed and definitely worth catching, and you'll have to cancel sleep for the last two days of frantic action. On the Monday morning – the day on which the islands celebrate slave emancipation in 1834 – **Jouvert** (pronounced *jouvay*, and meaning daybreak) is a huge jump-up party starting at 4am, while the Judging of the Bands competition in the afternoon sees the ranks of brightly costumed marching bands and floats parading through the city streets, being marked for colour, sound and general party attitude.

Tuesday has a final costumed parade through the streets, finishing with the announcement of all of the winners and a roughly 6pm-midnight last lap from Carnival City – "the bacchanal" – as the exhausted partygoers stream through St John's, led by the steelbands. All in all, it's a great event – certainly one of the best of the Caribbean's summer carnivals – and a great chance to catch the Antiguans in a non-stop party mood.

The city's main casino, packed with slot machines and offering blackjack, roulette and Caribbean stud poker tables for the more serious players. Live bands (Thurs–Sat) and karaoke (Sun) give the place a bit of atmosphere after 10pm. The casino will normally lay on one-way shuttle service to St John's for punters coming to town for the nights.

Pizzas in Paradise
Redcliffe Quay.
A funky atmosphere most of the week, with canned music and a crowd, indoors and out, most nights, and a live band on Thursdays.

Ribbit
Green Bay, ℗462 7996.
Just off the main road between St John's and Five Islands, Ribbit is alongside the Web as one of the island's two main nightclubs, popular with Antiguans and tourists alike and absolutely packed at the weekends. Music ranges from Jamaican dancehall to Eurosmooch, and the atmosphere is invariably welcoming.

Russell's
Fort James, St John's, ℗462 5479.
Sunday is the big day for music here, with loud merengue music in the early evening pulling a crowd of the island's Hispanics to twist on the dancefloor, and a more mellow jazz band from around 8pm.

Shooters
High St, St John's.
More pub than nightclub, but often open until the early hours and with plenty of loud music and the occasional live band.

The Web
Old Parham Road.
Unpromising looking place, three kilometres east of St John's – a small green shack just off the main road – but always cooking at weekends with a mixture of dancehall, reggae, soul and the occasional burst of Europop. The dancefloor is tiny and the whole place is pitch black but, for a bit of nightclubbing Antiguan-style, it's unmissable.

ENGLISH HARBOUR AND THE SOUTH

Abracadabra
English Harbour.
Welcoming place with open-air dancing to canned music on Tues and Fri and live Latin sounds on Sat.

The Last Lemming
Nelson's Dockyard.
Lively bar, often open later than anywhere else and with the occasional local band.

The Lookout
Shirley Heights (see pp.67–69).
Steel and reggae bands set up on the Heights on Sunday afternoons, overlooking English Harbour. There's a bar and barbecue, vendors selling trinkets and T-shirts and a great party atmosphere, though at the peak of the season you'll find little room to move.

Sports

The confirmed beach addict and the watersports fanatic are equally at home in Antigua, with a variety of great beaches to choose from and plenty of operators offering excellent **diving**, **snorkelling**, **waterskiing** and other activities. Also on the water, a number of companies offer **tours along the coast** by boat or catamaran, and you can charter boats for **deep sea fishing**. There are plenty of land-based options, too, with a couple of good **golf** courses, **horse-riding** stables and occasional **hiking** and **mountain-biking** trips.

Although diving (see opposite) is excellent in the south, the northwest coast is probably the best spot for general watersports, with Dickenson Bay in particular offering several reputable operators at its northern end. The sea is pretty calm here year round and, beyond the protected swimming zone, you can waterski, windsurf, parasail or rent jetskis. Paradise Reef, a half-kilometre-long coral garden to the north of the bay, is a popular spot for glass-bottom boat trips and snorkelling, and there are good coralheads offshore around tiny Prickly Pear Island.

Barbuda just about surpasses Antigua in the quality (and the quietness) of its beaches, and its snorkelling and diving opportunities are also world-class. Unfortunately, the island doesn't yet have the infrastructure to support tourists looking for watersports, so you'll have to take your own gear.

DIVING AND SNORKELLING

Diving is excellent on the coral reefs around Antigua and Barbuda, with most of the good sites – places like Sunken Rock and Cape Shirley – on the south of the island and many of them very close to shore, rarely more than a 10-15 minute boat-ride away. Expect to see a wealth of fabulously colourful reef fish, including parrot fish, angel fish, wrasse and barracuda, as well as the occasional harmless nurse shark and, if you're lucky, dolphins and turtles. The reefs for the most part are still in pristine, unspoiled condition, and, though there is no wall diving, there are some good cliffs and canyons and a handful of wrecks.

Antigua has plenty of reputable dive operators (see pp.122–123), scattered conveniently around so you should always be able to find a boat going out from near where you're staying. Rates are pretty uniform: reckon on around US$45 for a single-tank dive, US$65–70 for a two-tank dive and US$50–60 for a night dive. Beginners can get a feel for diving by taking a half-day **resort course**, involving basic theory, a shallow water (or pool) demonstration and a single dive. The course costs around US$80-100, and allows you to continue to dive with the people who taught you, though not with any other operator. Full **open water certification** – involving theory, tests, training dives and four full dives – is rather more variable in price, costing US$400–500, depending on the time of year and how busy the operator is. Call around for the best deal.

Serious divers should consider a **package deal**, either involving a simple 3 or 5 two-tank dive package (roughly US$180–200 and US$265–305 respectively) or a deal that includes accommodation and diving. Prices for these can be pretty good value, particularly outside the winter season – *Octopus Divers* and the *Galleon Beach Club*, for example, offer a week's accommodation and diving for around

US$700 per person – and it's worth contacting the dive operators direct to find out the latest offers.

Barbuda's diving is at least as good as Antigua's, with countless wrecks dotted around the nearby reefs, but, sadly, there is no established dive outfit on the island at the time of writing. If you're interested, it's worth asking some of the Antiguan dive operators for the latest information, or check with one of the agencies that offers tours to the island – they can normally arrange for certified divers to be provided with tanks and guides on Barbuda, though the costs can be hefty.

Snorkelling around the islands is excellent, too, and several of the dive operators take snorkellers on their dive trips, mooring near some good snorkellable coralheads. Reckon on around US$15-20 for an outing, including equipment, though if you're with a friend who's diving you may be able to blag yourself a free trip. However, a boat-ride is far from essential for snorkellers – there are loads of good spots just a short swim offshore from both Antigua and Barbuda, and these are mentioned throughout the Guide. Most of the top hotels have snorkelling gear for hire or loan, but if you're not at one of these, finding the equipment can be tricky, and it's worth bringing a mask and fins with you, certainly if you're heading to Barbuda.

Aquanauts

Map 2, D6. *St James Club*, Mamora Bay, ℭ460 5000.
Good, professional south coast outfit with top-quality equipment, catering for the hotel guests and drop-ins from elsewhere.

Dive Antigua

Map 4, F3. *Rex Halcyon Cove Hotel*, Dickenson Bay, ℭ462 3483, fax 462 7787.
The longest established and best-known dive operation on the island, based on the northwest coast, though prices are

normally 5–10 percent higher than most of the others. They offer a glass-bottomed boat to take snorkellers out to the reef.

Dockyard Divers

Map 5, E5. Nelson's Dockyard, ©460 1178, fax 460 1179.

Decent-sized dive shop, the only outfit in the English Harbour area offering snorkelling and diving trips around the south and west coasts.

Jolly Divers

Map 2, G5. *Club Antigua*, Jolly Harbour Marina, ©462 8305.

Second oldest diveshop in Antigua and, based at the enormous *Club Antigua*, one of the busiest. Look elsewhere if you want to go out in a small group.

Octopus Divers

Map 5, C1. Falmouth Harbour, ©460 6286, fax 463 8528.

New outfit with one of the most comfortable dive boats on the south coast, and some good-value hotel/diving package deals. No snorkelling offered.

Pirate Divers

Map 2, E2. *Lord Nelson's Beach Hotel*, Dutchman's Bay, ©46 3094.

Not the best location, on the often choppy northeast coast, requiring longer boat rides to many of the good sites, but a friendly operation and slightly lower costs than most of the others.

BOATS AND CATAMARANS

There is no shortage of boat and catamaran trips to be made around Antigua, with the emphasis – not, it must be said, everyone's cup of tea – normally on being part of a big crowd all having a fun time together. Most of the cruises charge a single price, including a meal and all the drinks you want, and the two main cruise companies, *Kokomo* and *Wadadli Cats*, offer virtually identical trips to various parts of the island, travelling on large and comfortable catamarans.

The most popular cruise – a great way to see the island – sails right round Antigua, taking in some snorkelling and lunch at Green Island off the east coast. There is also a superb snorkelling trip to Cades Reef on the south coast, stopping off for lunch on one of the west coast beaches, and another to uninhabited Great Bird Island – replete with plenty of birdlife – off the northeast. Finally, there's a "triple destination" cruise on Sundays to English Harbour via Green Island, ending with a taxi-ride up to the steel band party on Shirley Heights (see pp.67–69) and another taxi home.

Each of the trips picks up passengers from a number of different locations on the west coast, and all are out from around 9am until 4pm, apart from the Shirley Heights tour (roughly 9am–6.30pm). The circumnavigation cruise costs US$75 per person, Cades Reef US$60, and the triple destination cruise US$85, all prices including snorkelling gear, a buffet lunch and an open bar.

Coral Ark
©462 2248.
Day- and night-time boat cruises from St John's, usually heading to one of the west coast beaches where you can snorkel offshore or crash out in the sun.

Jolly Roger Pirate Cruises
©462 2064.
Hearty party cruises, with rope-swinging and walking the plank for those piratically inclined and limbo competitions and calypso dance classes for the rest.

Kokomo Cats
©462 7245.
Round the island trips (Tues, Thurs, Sat), Cades Reef (Fri), Great Bird Island (Wed), and English Harbour/Shirley Heights (Sun). They also offer sunset cruises (Tues, Thurs, Sat) from *Club Antigua* on the west coast, out from 6.30–9pm (US$30).

Wadadli Cats
©462 4792.
Circumnavigation cruises (Mon, Wed, Sat), Cades Reef (Wed), Great Bird Island (Tues-Fri) and English Harbour/Shirley Heights (Sun).

SAILING

Antigua is one of the prime sailing destinations in the Caribbean and, particularly during sailing week in April, it sometimes feels that the island is a refuelling and party stop for crowds of hearty yachters. If you're after some crewing on boats sailing between the West Indian islands, ask around and look out for crew notices at Nelson's dockyard on the south coast and at the yacht charter outfits (Sun Charters and Nicholsons) just outside the dockyard.

FISHING

Various charter boats offer deep-sea fishing trips where you can go after wahoo, tuna, barracuda and, if you're lucky, marlin and other sailfish. Prices for up to six people start at around US$250 for a half-day, $500 for a whole day, including rods, bait, food, drink and transport from your hotel. If you want to go on your own, operators will put you with another group if they can and charge around $100 for a half-day. Regular operators include Lobster King at Jolly Harbour (©462 4363), Obsession (©462 3174), and

Sailing week

Begun in 1967 with a tiny fleet of wooden fishing boats, and now regularly graced by over 200 quality yachts, the **English Harbour Race** is the centrepiece of Antigua's sailing week, a festival of racing and partying that transforms the area around Nelson's dockyard into a colourful and crowded carnival village and the harbour into a parking area for every type of sailing boat. Don't expect to find a lot of Antiguans present – its predominantly a party for the American and European sailing contingent – but if you're on the island in late April/early May it's a good place to see some superb sailing action and squeeze in a heavy night of bar-hopping.

Shorty's at Dickenson Bay (℡462 3626), but if you hunt around at dockside, particularly in St John's and Jolly Harbour, you can find plenty of others.

If you just want to go out with some local fishermen – which can be an amazing experience – ask around at one of the main fishing settlements like Old Road on the south coast. Many will be grateful for an extra pair of hands, though you'll need to clarify in advance exactly what's expected of you – pulling lobster pots and fishing nets is extremely tough work and you may be at it for hours.

OTHER WATERSPORTS

Many of the hotels have their own windsurfers which you can borrow for no extra cost, and there's a windsurfing school (daily 9am–5pm) at the Lord Nelson Beach Club (℡462 3094) on the northeast coast. Lessons are expensive at US$50 an hour; board rental costs US$225 for a week,

US$55 for a day and US$40 for half a day. Their bi-annual windsurfing regatta attracts serious surfers from around the world.

On Dickenson Bay, Halcyon Cove Watersports (at the *Rex Halcyon Cove Hotel*, ✆462 0256) and Sea Sports (✆462 3355) offer a variety of watersports. A ten-minute parasail costs US$45, a similar period of waterskiing costs US$25, while jet-skis cost US$30 for half an hour (US$40 for a two-seater). You'll also find various guys offering you use of their jet-skis and small sailboats at negotiable prices; it usually works out cheaper than going with an established company but bear in mind that insurance will be non-existent.

GOLF

There are two eighteen-hole public **golf courses** in Antigua, although the tourist maps seem to claim many more. Ten minutes' drive north of St John's, the Cedar Valley Golf Club (✆462 0161) is a 5932 yard, par 69 championship course, venue for the annual Antigua Open, held each November. It's a lovely course, lined with palms, flamboyants and cedars and, from its higher points, offers great panoramic views of the island. Given the dryness of the islands, water hazards are mercifully few but, that aside, it's a reasonably challenging course. Green fees are US$34 for eighteen holes, (US$17 for nine holes), plus US$10 per person for rental of clubs and another US$34 if you want to rent a cart (US$17 for 9 holes). The dress code is pretty relaxed, but you will need a collared shirt.

The **Jolly Harbour Golf Course** (✆480 6950) is the island's other major golf location, a newly opened par 71 course designed by American Karl Litten. It's a decent course, though flatter and less attractive than Cedar Valley, and costs around US$40 for eighteen holes.

GOLF

HORSERIDING

Though you'll probably be offered a horseback tour during your visit (often, sadly, on a rather mangy and forlorn creature), there is only one official **horseriding** stables on the island, located just west of Falmouth at Spring Hill (℡460 1775 or 463 8041). They have around a dozen horses and offer lessons for EC$50 per hour or simple riding tours of the area for EC$40 per hour.

TENNIS AND SQUASH

Many of the hotels have their own tennis courts, best at places like *Royal Antiguan* and the *St James Club*, but there are public tennis and squash courts available around the island, charging around EC$35 for an hour, and EC$10 for hire of equipment

BBR Sportif

Map 2, G5. Jolly Harbour, ℡462 6260.
Private squash and tennis courts at this exclusive west coast resort; rackets and other equipment can be hired.

Temo Sports

Map 5, G1. Falmouth Harbour, ℡460 1781.
Squash and tennis courts, with all equipment available for hire.

Directory

All services listed are in
St John's unless otherwise stated.

Airlines American Airlines ✆ 462 0952; British Airways
✆ 462 0876; LIAT, High St/Corn Alley ✆ 480 5850.

Ambulance Emergency ✆ 462 0251.

American Express Corner of Long St/Thames St ✆ 462 4788,
open Mon–Thurs 8.30am–4.30pm, Fri 8.30am–5pm.

Banks St John's: Antigua Commercial Bank, St Mary's/Thames St
Mon–Thurs 8am–2pm, Fri 8am–5pm; Bank of Antigua,
Thames/High St Mon–Thurs 8am–3pm, Fri 8am–4pm, Sat
8am–1pm; Barclays, High/Market St Mon–Thurs 8am–2pm, Fri
8am–4pm; ABIB, Woods Centre Mon–Fri 9am–4pm, Sat
9am–1pm. **English Harbour:** Mon–Thurs & Sat 9am–1pm, Fri
9am–noon & 2–4pm.

Dentists Antigua Barbuda Dental Group, Newgate St ✆ 460 3368;
Dr Maxwell Francis, Cross/Newgate St ✆ 462 0058;
Dr Sengupta, Woods Centre ✆ 462 9312.

Embassies British High Commission, 11 Old Parham Rd
✆ 462 0008; US Embassy, Queen Elizabeth Highway ✆ 462 3505.

Film Island Photo, Redcliffe/Market St, sells film and does 1 hour photo development; Benjie's, Heritage Quay, offers the same service and has various camera accessories at duty-free prices.

Hospitals Holbertson Public Hospital, Hospital Road ✆ 462 0251; Adelin Medical Centre, Fort Road ✆ 462 0866.

Laundry Burton's, Camacho Avenue ✆ 462 4268; O'Beez Laundromat, Factory Road ✆ 462 4661.

Newspapers First Edition, Woods Centre Mon–Sat 9am–9pm, gets some US newspapers and the British Sunday papers one day late.

Pharmacies Full service pharmacies at Benjies, Redcliffe / Market St ✆ 462 0723, Mon–Wed 8.30am–5pm, Thurs & Sat 8.30am–4pm, Fri 8.30-5.30pm and Woods, Woods Centre Mon–Sat 9am–10pm, Sun 11am–6pm.

Police The main police station in town is on Newgate St, ✆ 462 0045. Emergency ✆ 462 0125 or ✆ 999 or ✆ 911.

Post Office St John's: Long St Mon–Fri 8.15am–4pm; Woods Centre Mon–Thurs 8.30am–4pm, Fri 8.30am–5pm. **English Harbour:** Mon–Fri 8.30am–4pm

Taxis West Bus Station Taxis ✆ 462 5190, Dion's Taxis ✆ 462 3466, and Reliable Taxis ✆ 462 1510.

Telephone Cable & Wireless, St Mary's St, have facilities for making overseas calls.

Travel Agents Bryson's, corner of Long St & Thames St ✆ 480 1230, is open Mon–Fri 8am–4pm, Sat 8am–noon.

DIRECTORY

CONTEXTS

A brief history of Antigua and Barbuda

Antigua's **first people** were the Siboney, originally from present-day Venezuela in South America, and the earliest traces of their presence date from around 3100 BC. They were simple, nomadic people who used flint and shell to make tools and collected fish and conch from the shallow waters around the islands. By the early years AD the Siboney had been replaced by Arawak-speaking **Amerindians** from the same region, peaceful, farming people who made and traded pottery and introduced plants like cassava, pineapple and tobacco; they in turn were beginning to be supplanted by the more warlike **Carib** Indians – who called the island Wadadli – around the time of Christopher Columbus.

Barbuda's history has taken a somewhat different course from Antigua's over the last 500 years – see p.77 for more information.

The first European sighting of Antigua came on November 11, 1493 when **Columbus**, on his second voyage of "discovery", sailed close by. He named the island Santa Maria la Antigua after a miracle-working shrine in Seville, where he had prayed before beginning his journey from Spain. Neither Columbus nor his sailors set foot on the heavily wooded island, pressing on instead for the supposed riches to be found further west. In 1525, a small party of Spanish settlers did make it to the island, but harassment from Carib Indians and a shortage of fresh water sources soon drove them off, and the island was left untouched for a century.

In 1624, the first **English settlement** in the West Indies was established on the island of St Kitts, and the English also laid nominal claim to nearby Antigua and Barbuda. Eight years later, a party of English sailors landed on Antigua, founding a settlement at Falmouth on the south coast. These settlers had come to the West Indies to make money from farming, and they experimented with a number of crops – notably tobacco, cotton and indigo – before settling on **sugar**, which was to guarantee the island its future wealth.

Sugarcane was introduced to the Caribbean from Brazil, which supplied 80 percent of the European sugar market during the 1630s. With Brazilian exports disrupted by civil war during the 1640s, an opportunity arose for the West Indian islands – where sugar grew exceptionally well – to feed some of the booming demand for the stuff. Barbados was the first island to seize the opportunity, and Antigua followed soon after with its own mini sugar boom. The population jumped from 750 in 1646 to 1200 a decade later.

Sugar becomes king

By the beginning of the eighteenth century, the Caribs had all been driven off or killed, and sugar was fast becoming king in Antigua. Christopher Codrington's Betty's Hope plantation (see p.55) was a model sugar estate, with all the latest technology, and its success drew more sugar entrepreneurs out from Britain. As they arrived, they cleared their own patch of native forest and the island was gradually denuded of vegetation other than the ubiquitous sugarcane. By 1706 there were 27 sugar mills in Antigua, by 1710 there were 74 and by 1748 there were as many as 175. For 200 years, sugar was to remain far and away the country's dominant industry, bringing enormous wealth to the **planters**, who ran their estates like their personal fiefdoms.

Naturally, other countries looked on this success with envy. Colonial wars between the main European powers were regular events from the mid-seventeenth through to the early nineteenth centuries, and most of Britain's West Indian colonies changed hands as many as a dozen times. In part because of its success, Antigua was unusual. Although St John's was destroyed by a **French invasion** in 1666, Antigua never actually fell into French or Dutch hands. This was due, in large part, to the massive fortifications built around the island, with forty separate defences erected, the major ones at places like Monks Hill (see p.61) and Shirley Heights (see p.67) on the south coast.

Slavery

The success of the sugar industry, and the wealth of the planters, was of course built upon the appalling inhumanity of **slavery**. Development of the estates required a huge workforce and, with no indigenous population, the only option the planters could envisage was the importation of slaves from Africa, a business which had already been in existence for many years, providing labour throughout the Americas.

The slave trade was dominated by British merchants. Their ships sailed first to the west coast of Africa – from where most of the slaves were taken – carrying trinkets and other goods to barter for the human cargo. From Africa many of the ships sailed to Jamaica – the most important transhipment point in the region – where the slaves were unloaded into warehouses and sold at auction. The slaves were then sent on to islands like Antigua and Barbados, while the ships would return to Britain, now laden with West Indian products like rum, sugar and spices.

This **triangular trade** brought great riches to the traders, reflected in the development of major British ports like Bristol and Liverpool, but scant attention was paid to the plight of the West Africans. Many were taken prisoner in the heart of their continent, marched hundreds of miles to stockades on the coast and then chained and crammed into the holds of a stinking ship for six to twelve weeks with little room to stretch their limbs, let alone any sanitation facilities. Many died of disease or malnutrition; many others committed suicide if the chance arose, sometimes leaping from the ship rather than continue in captivity.

On arrival in the colonies, the slaves found conditions mostly squalid with little living space or privacy on the sugar estates. Conditions were better in **Barbuda**, where sugar never took hold and slaves worked more as herdsmen and small farmers, but in Antigua the toil of the plantations was relentless, and the whims of the overseers often unimaginably cruel.

Naturally, particularly in the early years, there was **resistance** from the slaves. Runaways fled for the island's woods and the hills around Boggy Peak, but there were few mountainous areas for them to hide and they were easily hunted down. Punishment was swift and brutal. 1736 saw the most serious planning for a slave revolt, with a plot to kill all of the whites in St John's uncovered at the last minute; all of the rebel leaders were executed as a deterrent to those who thought to follow their example. Nonetheless, the plot increased fear among the white population – already massively outnumbered by blacks – and led to increasingly repressive treatment of slaves.

Emancipation

As time went by, conditions for the slaves slowly improved. Religious conversion played a part in this, with Moravian and Methodist **missionaries** coming to Antigua to preach among and help to educate the slaves. Conversion encouraged slave-owners to treat slaves as human for the first time and they even began to give them Sundays off to attend church. In 1807 Britain abolished the slave trade and, in 1834, the Act of Emancipation was passed, and all of the island's 29,000 slaves declared to be free men and women.

Perhaps inevitably, the joy of emancipation soon turned to despair as the freed slaves realized their economic predicament. Unlike Jamaica, which encompassed great tracts of unused land on which former slaves could establish smallholdings, Antigua was almost entirely covered in sugar plantations. Some of the ex-slaves headed for St John's but, with nowhere else to work, many were obliged to continue to labour at the sugar estates and found wages insufficient to provide even the miserly levels of food, housing and care offered under slavery. In particular, the plantation owners no longer felt bound to provide for the very young, the old and the sick, and the numbers of destitute people rose precipitately.

Gradually, though, **free villages** began to emerge at places like Liberta, Jennings and Bendals, often based around Moravian or Methodist churches or on land reluctantly sold by the planters to a group of former slaves. By 1840 there were around thirty such villages, and slowly a few Antiguans scratched together sufficient money to set up their own businesses – shops, taverns and tiny cottage industries. An embryonic black middle class was in the making.

The islands sink into decline

By the mid-nineteenth century the sugar industry was entering a crisis, largely induced by the drop in European sugar prices that followed the introduction of home-produced sugar beet, and aggravated by local droughts and hurricanes. Planters went bankrupt and were forced to sell off their land to local merchants and financial institutions. For a century there was little progress on the island.

By the time of World War II, life for the vast majority of Antiguans was still extremely tough. There was widespread poverty across the island while, for those who had did have work on the plantations, hours were long and conditions onerous. In 1938, the **Moyne Commission** was sent from London to report on social conditions in the West Indies, and recorded that Antigua was among the most impoverished and neglected islands in the region. It recommended reform to the island's stringent laws banning trade unions, and in the following year the **Antigua Trades and Labour Union** was formed.

Within a few years the union had helped to improve conditions for plantation workers. Its major success came in 1951 when, under the leadership of former Salvation Army officer **Vere (V.C.) Bird,** workers refused to handle the sugar crop until their rates of pay were improved. For a year, the employers tried to starve the workers into submission, but they were eventually forced to concede a substantial pay rise. National confidence began to improve.

The road to independence

After the war, Antigua continued to be administered from afar by Britain's colonial office, but gradually the island's fledgling politicians were given authority for the day-to-day running of their country. The **Antigua Labour Party** (an offshoot of the ATLU) won the first local **elections** in 1946, and a decade later the island was given responsible ministerial government. Ideological differences between the political parties were minimal, and all parties quickly came to support some sort of independence from Britain. A constitutional conference was held in 1966, leading the following year to autonomy for the country in its internal and foreign affairs, although defence remained a matter for Britain.

Slowly, the national economy began to take strides forward, assisted (despite the closure of the last sugar plantations in 1971) by the development of tourism. By the elections of 1980 all parties considered that, politically and economically, the country was sufficiently mature for full independence and, following a further conference in Britain, the flag of an **independent Antigua and Barbuda** was finally raised in November 1981.

The Bird dynasty

After taking over the leadership of the ATLU in 1943, V.C. Bird dominated Antiguan politics for half a century. Known as Papa Bird, he became the colony's first chief minister in 1956, its first premier in 1967 when internal self-government was granted by Britain, and the first prime minister of an independent Antigua and Barbuda in 1981.

Bird (and his entourage) have been consistently controversial. Hugely popular with ordinary Antiguans, he and his government developed a reputation for doing business with all kinds of dodgy characters. There were allegations that ministers had brokered arms deals between Israel and the apartheid regime in South Africa, and even with the Medellin drugs cartel in Colombia. A British commission accused the government of "unbridled corruption", and the USA – who kept a military base on the island and poured in over US$200 million in aid – of turning a blind eye, in an era when fear of radical governments (such as those of Cuba and Grenada) was its leading concern.

Antigua today

Whatever the truth of the allegations, Vere Bird retained power until 1994 when, at the age of 84, he handed leadership of his party and the country to his giant son Lester, once Antigua's leading fast bowler and now probably its wealthiest man. Bird's government has continued to promote tourism (badly dented by the catastrophic hurricane of 1995) as the country's economic dynamo, despite increasing fears for the consequent ecological impact.

Farming (fruit, vegetables and livestock) and light manufacturing continue to provide some diversification for the islands, but a third of the working population are employed by hotels and restaurants, and tourism accounts for about 60 percent of foreign exchange earnings. As a result, Antigua's biggest fear (as with most islands in the region) is that it has put all of its eggs in one basket; should tourism dry up, the country risks being left without any economic lifeline. For now, though, prosperity appears to be still on the rise as the nation heads into the new millenium.

Cricket

If you're in Antigua for any length of time, you'll find it almost impossible to avoid the subject of **cricket** – the true national passion. If you're lucky, there'll be a game at the Antigua Recreation Ground in St John's during your stay; if so, don't miss the chance to get along and check out the calypso atmosphere. Failing that, expect at least to get roped into a game of beach cricket, where you'll find fielders standing under the palm trees and in the sea waiting for a miscued shot.

Cricket arrived in Antigua via the British military in the mid-nineteenth century. The 59th Foot Regiment formed the island's first club on New Year's Day 1842, and the Antigua Times recorded an Antigua XI beaten by the crew of *HMS Phaeton* at Shirley Heights on September 26, 1863. For decades, cricket clubs remained the preserve of the ruling class: strictly whites-only and often little more than extended social clubs for the planters and merchants. But, despite the early snobbery that was attached to the game, it soon began to catch on in the sugar estates, where the workers drew up their own pitches and organized their own matches.

In 1895 Antigua received its first overseas touring team, who reported playing against a home team composed entirely of "coloured" players. (On the same tour, by comparison, the authorities in Barbados excluded black players from their team, irrespective of merit.) In 1920 the Rising Sun Cricket Club was founded for poor men in St John's, and by the 1930s – half a century before independence – Antigua had its first black sporting hero in the batsman **Pat Nanton**.

Nonetheless, Antigua remained a cricketing minnow well into the twentieth century, with the regional game dominated by the "Big Four" cricket nations: Jamaica, Barbados, Trinidad and Guyana. In 1966 the Caribbean Shell Shield competition was established for those four and a fifth team – the Combined Islands – made up of players from Antigua and the other small islands. Rarely taken seriously during the 1970s, this Combined Islands team swept to victory in the Shield in 1981, the year of Antigua's independence, led by the brilliant Antiguan **Viv Richards** (see p.46). From that time, the Combined Islands team was allowed to become two – the Leeward Islands of the northeastern Caribbean (dominated by Antigua) and the Windward Islands of the southeast (including Grenada, St Vincent and St Lucia) – with the Leewards team consistently performing well in both the Shield and the one-day Red Stripe Cup, inaugurated in 1982.

The first Antiguan to play for the West Indies team was fast bowler **Andy Roberts**, who made his debut against England in 1974; he was shortly followed by Richards, who first played against India in the same year. Within a couple of years both players had made a dramatic impact on the side – heavily involved in the slaughter of English cricket in 1976 – and their success lent considerable weight to their country's growing self-confidence in the run-up to independence. In 1981 the island was awarded the right to stage its first Test Match, where Richards made a superb and entirely predictable century.

The rules of cricket

The **rules of cricket** are so complex that the official rule book runs to some twenty pages. The basics, however, are by no means as Byzantine as the game's detractors make out.

There are two teams of eleven players. A team wins by scoring more runs than the other team and dismissing all the opposition – in other words, a team could score many runs more than the opposition, but still not win if the last enemy batsman doggedly stays "in" (hence ensuring a draw). The match is divided into innings, when one team bats and the other fields. The number of innings varies depending on the type of competition: one-day matches have one per team, Test matches have two.

The aim of the fielding side is to limit the runs scored and get the batsmen "out". Two players from the batting side are on the pitch at any one time. The bowling side has a bowler, a wicket keeper and nine fielders. Two umpires, one standing behind the stumps at the bowler's end and one square on to the play, are responsible for adjudicating if a batsman is out. Each innings is divided into overs, consisting of six deliveries, after which the wicket keeper changes ends, the bowler is changed and the fielders move positions.

The batsmen score runs either by running up and down from wicket to wicket (one length = one run), or by hitting the ball over the boundary rope, scoring four runs if it crosses the boundary having touched the ground, and six runs if it flies over. The main ways a batsman can be dismissed are: by being "clean bowled", where the bowler dislodges the bails of the wicket (the horizontal pieces of wood resting on top of the stumps); by being "run out", which is when one of the fielding side dislodges the bails with the ball while the batsman is running between the wickets; by being caught, which is when any of the fielding side catches the ball after the batsman has hit it and before it touches the ground; or "LBW" (leg before wicket), where the batsman blocks with his leg a delivery that would otherwise have hit his stumps.

These are the bare rudiments of a game whose beauty lies in the subtlety of its skills and tactics. The captain, for example, chooses which bowler to play and where to position his fielders to counter the strengths of the batsman, the condition of the pitch and a dozen other variables. Cricket also has a beauty in its esoteric language, used to describe such things as fielding positions ("silly mid-off", "cover point", etc) and the various types of bowling delivery ("googly", "yorker", etc).

Today, unthinkable just two decades ago, tiny Antigua is one of the leading cricketing venues in the Caribbean, with Test matches, Shell Shield and Red Stripe Cup games played there annually. Between 1985 and 1995 the West Indies team was captained by Antiguans – Richards and, later, his protégé Richie Richardson – and Antiguan players like Curtley Ambrose continue to dominate on the world cricketing stage. Small wonder, perhaps, that at times people appear to talk of little else.

Books

Several of the harder to find books described below are available at the national museum in St John's.

Brian Dyde, *Antigua and Barbuda* (Macmillan). Excellent introduction to the islands, with chapters on everything from history and natural history to the economy and the main tourist sights.

Vincent Harlow, *Christopher Codrington 1669–1710* (Oxford University Press). Not easy to get hold of, but a fascinating biography of Antigua's first sugar-baron, who was also the "founder" of Barbuda.

Eugene Kaplan, *Field guide to the coral reefs of the Caribbean* (Peterson's). Useful introduction to everything you'll find in the sea around Antigua.

Jamaica Kincaid, *A Small Place* (Vintage). Antigua's most famous and now self-exiled novelist.

George Lamming, *In the Castle of my Skin* (Longman). One of the outstanding Caribbean novels, by a leading author from Barbados, evoking a nostalgic and beautifully described picture of the West Indies that belonged to former generations.

Patrick Leigh Fermor, *The Traveller's Tree* (Penguin). The classic Caribbean travelogue describing the author's visit in the 1940s, before tourism had really started in the region, though only one of the chapters covers his time on Antigua.

G.W. Lennox & S.A. Seddon, *Flowers of the Caribbean* and *Trees of the Caribbean* (both Macmillan). Handy pocket-sized books, with glossy, sharp, colour pictures, and a good general introduction to the region's flora.

Trevor McDonald, *Viv Richards* (Sphere). Excellent little biography of Antigua's finest cricketer, offering a useful overview of the game during the era of Kerry Packer and the emergence of the West Indies as the world's leading team.

Michael Manley, *A History of West Indies Cricket* (Deutsch). A superb history of the Caribbean contribution to the world's greatest game, engagingly written by the late prime minister of Jamaica.

Reynolds Morse, *The Quest for M.P. Shiel's Realm of Redonda* (Cleveland). The bizarre story of the kings of uninhabited Redonda (see p.84).

Desmond Nicholson, *Antigua, Barbuda & Redonda – a Historical Sketch, Forts of Antigua & Barbuda, The Story of the Arawaks* (all Museum of Antigua and Barbuda). Superbly researched studies of the island by Antigua's leading historian.

J.P. Parry, Philip Sherlock & Anthony Maingot, *A short history of the West Indies* (Macmillan). The best concise history of the region, taking the story up on the mid-1980s and good on general issues like regional co-operation and debt crisis.

A Small Place

Savage and satirical, A Small Place is author **Jamaica Kincaid's** polemic on the corruption of her country at the hands of its colonial and present-day rulers. Don't expect to find the book in Antigua; its sale is banned to avoid distress to the venal politicians and patronizing tourists who draw equal fire from her pen. Barbed as it is, though, the book makes for an invigorating and provocative read, the complaint of a small girl who lived on a street named after an English "maritime criminal" (Nelson Street) and grew up to see roads being repaired for the visit of the Queen from England, and government ministers flying off for medical treatment in New York while the Antiguan hospitals were left understaffed and underfunded.

Polly Patullo, *Last Resorts – the Cost of Tourism in the Caribbean* (Cassell). Important, well-researched critique of the tourist industry and its impact on the islands.

David Schwab (ed), *Caribbean, the Lesser Antilles – the Insight Guide* (APA). Glossy guide to the eastern Caribbean, short on practical information but long on colour photographs and features, making it a decent souvenir book.

Keithlyn Smith & Fernando Smith, *To Shoot Hard Labour (the Life and Times of Samuel Smith, an Antiguan Workingman 1877–1982)* (Karia Press). Graphic and often poignant account of life in Antigua during and after slavery.

INDEX

Stay in touch with us!

ROUGH*NEWS* is Rough Guides' free newsletter.
In three issues a year we give you news, travel issues, music reviews, readers' letters and the latest dispatches from authors on the road.

I would like to receive ROUGH*NEWS*: please put me on your free mailing list.

NAME . . . .

ADDRESS . . . .

Please clip or photocopy and send to: Rough Guides, 1 Mercer Street, London WC2H 9QJ, England

or Rough Guides, 375 Hudson Street, New York, NY 10014, USA.

Backpacking through **Europe**?

Cruising across the **US of A**?

Clubbing in **London**?

Trekking through **Costa Rica**?

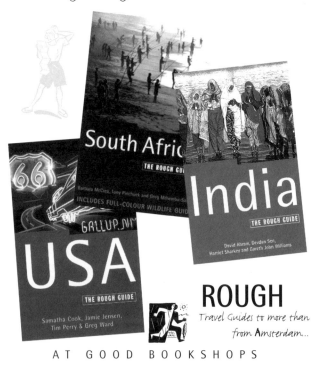

South Afric

Barbara McCrea, Tony Pinchuck and Greg Mthembu-S...

INCLUDES FULL-COLOUR WILDLIFE GUIDE

India

THE ROUGH GUIDE

David Abram, Devdan Sen,
Harriet Sharkey and Gareth John Williams

66

GALLUP,NM

USA

THE ROUGH GUIDE

Samatha Cook, Jamie Jensen,
Tim Perry & Greg Ward

ROUGH

Travel Guides to more than
from Amsterdam...

Wherever you're headed, **Rough Guides** tell you what's happening – the history, the people, the politics, the best beaches, nightlife and entertainment on your budget

Malaysia
Singapore & Brunei
THE ROUGH GUIDE

Australia
THE ROUGH GUIDE

Europe
THE ROUGH GUIDE
1999 EDITION
30 Countries • 100 Maps •
Includes Turkey, Morocco & the Baltic States

GUIDES
100 destinations worldwide
...to Zimbabwe.

DISTRIBUTED BY PENGUIN

IF KNOWLEDGE IS POWER, THIS ROUGH GUIDE IS A POCKET-SIZED BATTERING RAM

Written in plain English, with no hint of jargon, the Rough Guide to the Internet will make you an Internet guru in the shortest possible time. It cuts through the hype and makes all others look like nerdy textbooks

ROUGH GUIDES ON THE WEB

Visit our website www.roughguides.com for news about the latest books, online travel guides and updates, and the full text of our Rough Guide to Rock.

AT ALL BOOKSTORES • DISTRIBUTED BY PENGUIN

All great expeditions start here.

On-the-spot vaccinations plus travel healthcare advice. For your nearest Travel Clinic call **01276 685040.**

BRITISH AIRWAYS
TRAVEL CLINICS

TLA3

MAP LIST

MAP SYMBOLS

═══	Major road		◠	Cave
▭▭▭	Minor road		▲	Peak
───	Waterway		✈	Airport
†	Church		◼	Accommodation
✉	Post office		◉	Places to eat and drink
ⓘ	Information office		░	Beach
♜	Castle		▦	Park

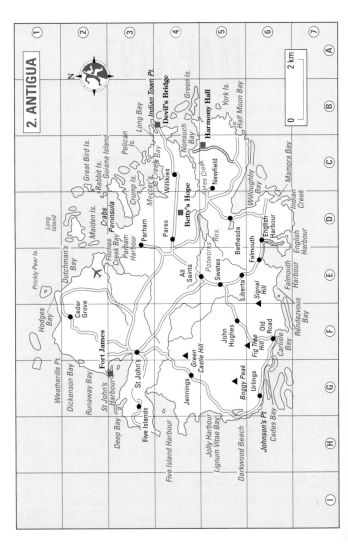

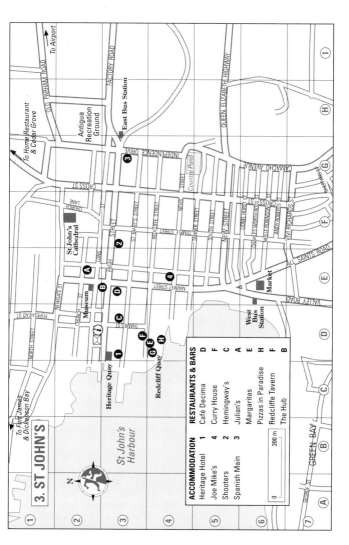

3. ST JOHN'S

St John's Harbour

ACCOMMODATION

Heritage Hotel	1
Joe Mike's	4
Shooters	2
Spanish Main	3

RESTAURANTS & BARS

Café Decima	D
Curry House	F
Hemingway's	C
Julian's	A
Margaritas	E
Pizzas in Paradise	H
Redcliffe Tavern	F
The Hub	B

0 ____ 200 m

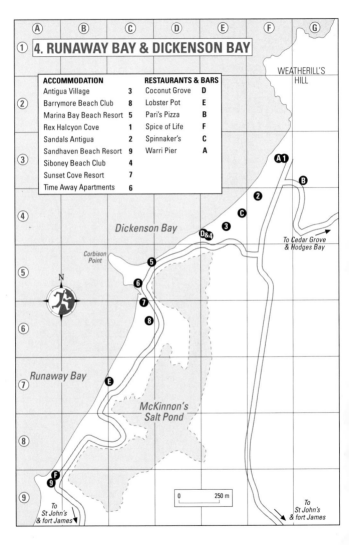

4. RUNAWAY BAY & DICKENSON BAY

WEATHERILL'S HILL

ACCOMMODATION

Antigua Village	3
Barrymore Beach Club	8
Marina Bay Beach Resort	5
Rex Halcyon Cove	1
Sandals Antigua	2
Sandhaven Beach Resort	9
Siboney Beach Club	4
Sunset Cove Resort	7
Time Away Apartments	6

RESTAURANTS & BARS

Coconut Grove	D
Lobster Pot	E
Pari's Pizza	B
Spice of Life	F
Spinnaker's	C
Warri Pier	A

Dickenson Bay

Corbison Point

To Cedar Grove & Hodges Bay

N

Runaway Bay

McKinnon's Salt Pond

0   250 m

To St John's & fort James

To St John's & fort James

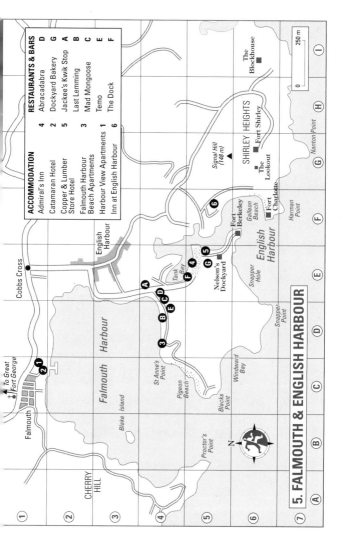

ACCOMMODATION

Admiral's Inn	4
Catamaran Hotel	2
Copper & Lumber Store Hotel	5
Falmouth Harbour Beach Apartments	3
Harbour View Apartments	1
Inn at English Harbour	6

RESTAURANTS & BARS

Abracadabra	D
Dockyard Bakery	G
Jackee's Kwik Stop	A
Last Lemming	B
Mad Mongoose	C
Temo	E
The Dock	F

250 m

5. FALMOUTH & ENGLISH HARBOUR

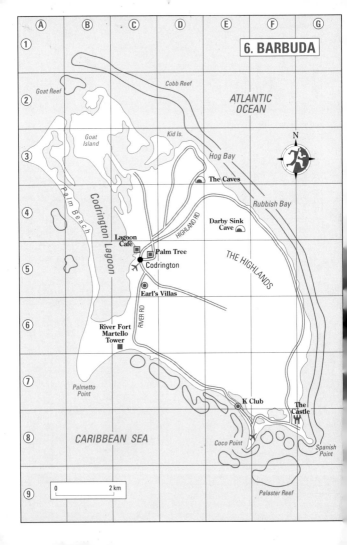